Mifflin
Harcourt

Science

Grade 7

Copyright © 2014 by Houghton Mifflin Harcourt Publishing Company

All rights reserved. No part of this work may be reproduced or transmitted in any form or by any means, electronic or mechanical, including photocopying or recording, or by any information storage or retrieval system, without the prior written permission of the copyright owner unless such copying is expressly permitted by federal copyright law.

Permission is hereby granted to individuals to photocopy entire pages from this publication in classroom quantities for instructional use and not for resale. Requests for information on other matters regarding duplication of this work should be addressed to Houghton Mifflin Harcourt Publishing Company, Attn: Contracts, Copyrights, and Licensing, 9400 Southpark Center Loop, Orlando, Florida 32819-8647.

Next Generation Science Standards and the associated logo are registered trademarks of Achieve, Inc. Neither Achieve nor the lead states and partners that developed the Next Generation Science Standards were involved in the production of this book, and they do not endorse it.

Printed in the U.S.A.

ISBN 978-0-544-26817-3

7 8 9 10 0982 22 21 20 19 18 17

4500651439 B C D E F G

If you have received these materials as examination copies free of charge, Houghton Mifflin Harcourt Publishing Company retains title to the materials and they may not be resold. Resale of examination copies is strictly prohibited.

Possession of this publication in print format does not entitle users to convert this publication, or any portion of it, into electronic format.

Core Skills Science
GRADE 7
Table of Contents

© Houghton Mifflin Harcourt Publishing Company

Introduction

The *Core Skills Science* series offers parents and educators high-quality, curriculum-based products that align with the Next Generation Science Standards* Disciplinary Core Ideas for grades 1–8. The *Core Skills Science* series provides informative and grade-appropriate readings on a wide variety of topics in life, earth, and physical science. Two pages of worksheets follow each reading passage. The book includes:

- clear illustrations, making scientific concepts accessible to young learners

- engaging reading passages, covering a wide variety of topics in life, earth, and physical science

- logically sequenced activities, transitioning smoothly from basic comprehension to higher-order thinking skills

- comprehension questions, ascertaining that students understand what they have read

- vocabulary activities, challenging students to show their understanding of scientific terms

- critical thinking activities, increasing students' ability to analyze, synthesize, and evaluate scientific information

- questions in standardized-test format, helping prepare students for state exams

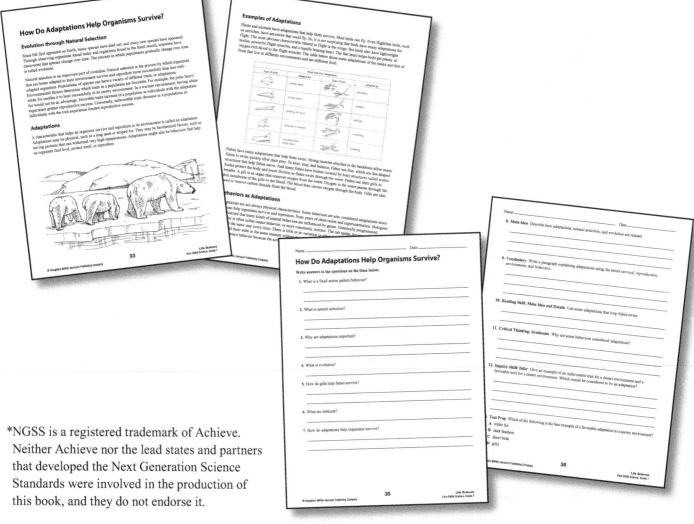

*NGSS is a registered trademark of Achieve. Neither Achieve nor the lead states and partners that developed the Next Generation Science Standards were involved in the production of this book, and they do not endorse it.

© Houghton Mifflin Harcourt Publishing Company

How Are Cell Structure and Function Related?

Cells and Living Things

Every living thing is composed of one or more cells. A cell is the structural and functional unit of life. This means it is the smallest unit that can carry out the activities of life, such as taking in nutrients, removing wastes, and reproducing. Unicellular organisms consist of only one cell. Multicellular organisms consist of many cells. Humans are multicellular organisms that consist of trillions of cells. In an organism made up of only one cell, different parts of the cell perform different functions. In an organism with many cells, different kinds of cells perform specialized functions. For example, red blood cells in humans specialize in delivering oxygen throughout the body. Cells have many different functions and come in many shapes and sizes. But all cells have some parts in common.

Prokaryotes and Eukaryotes

Although cells vary greatly in structure and function, all cells are one of two types: prokaryotic cell without a nucleus or eukaryotic cell with a nucleus. Prokaryotic and eukaryotic cells share several characteristics. Both have a cell membrane that encloses the cell and regulates the materials that enter and leave it. Inside the cell membrane, a fluid material, called cytoplasm, fills the cell. Most prokaryotic and eukaryotic cells also have ribosomes, where proteins are made. All cells also have DNA, which regulates cellular activities such as making proteins and reproduction. The DNA in a prokaryote floats around freely within the cell, while in the eukaryote, the DNA is held within the nucleus.

Cell Organelles

Cells have organelles that carry out many life processes. Organelles are structures that have specific jobs inside the cell. Different kinds of cells have different organelles, and this allows the cells to perform different functions. Most organelles are surrounded by membranes.

Eukaryotic cells have the same basic organelles.

- The nucleus is the organelle that contains the cell's DNA. The nucleus is the control center of the cell.
- A ribosome is a tiny organelle that manufactures proteins. Ribosomes do not have a membrane.
- A chloroplast is an organelle in plants that uses the energy of sunlight to make food.
- Mitochondria are organelles that break down food molecules to make energy carrier molecules called ATP.
- The endoplasmic reticulum makes lipids, breaks down drugs and other substances, and packages proteins for the Golgi complex.
- The Golgi complex processes and transports proteins and other materials out of a cell.
- Lysosomes contain enzymes that digest food particles, wastes, cell parts, and foreign invaders.
- The large central vacuole in plant cells stores water and other materials.
- The cytoskeleton is a network of proteins, such as microtubules and microfilaments, inside a cell that supports and shapes the cell.

1

Life Science
Core Skills Science, Grade 7

Plant cells also have an outermost structure called a cell well. A cell wall is a rigid structure that gives support to a cell. Plants and algae have cell walls made of a complex sugar called cellulose. Fungi, including yeasts and mushrooms, also have cell walls. Fungi have cell walls made of a complex sugar called chitin or of a chemical similar to chitin.

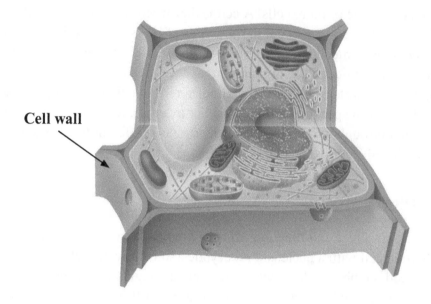

Cell wall

Tissues, Organs, and Organ Systems

The relationship between structure and function in organisms can extend past the cellular level. In multicellular organisms, specialized cells join together to form different types of tissue that perform specific functions. There are many types of tissue, including epithelial tissue, connective tissue, and muscle tissue. Different types of tissues can join together to form organs. Organs complete specific functions in an organism, such as eating or breathing. Organs can be joined into organ systems, and complex organisms are made up of many different organ systems.

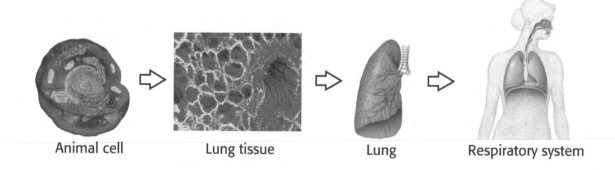

Animal cell   Lung tissue   Lung   Respiratory system

© Houghton Mifflin Harcourt Publishing Company

Name _____ Date _____

How Are Cell Structure and Function Related?

Match each definition to its term.

Definitions   **Terms**

_____ **1.** contains the cell's DNA   **a.** lysosome

_____ **2.** digests food particles   **b.** cell wall

_____ **3.** stores water and other materials in plants   **c.** cell membrane

_____ **4.** captures energy from sunlight to make food   **d.** central vacuole

_____ **5.** rigid structure that supports plant cells   **e.** nucleus

_____ **6.** protective barrier that encloses all cells   **f.** cytoskeleton

_____ **7.** a network of proteins that support and shape a cell   **g.** chloroplast

8. Main Idea Explain how structure and function are related in cells.

_____

_____

_____

_____

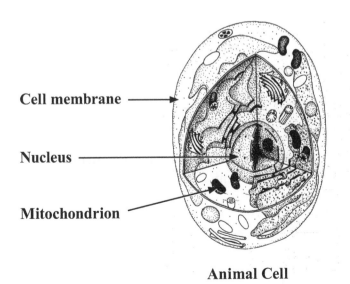

Animal Cell

Cell membrane

Nucleus

Mitochondrion

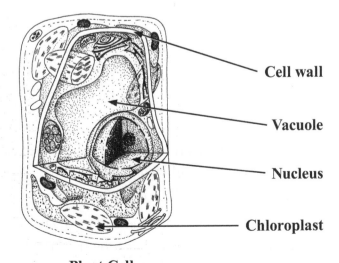

Plant Cell

Cell wall

Vacuole

Nucleus

Chloroplast

© Houghton Mifflin Harcourt Publishing Company

Life Science
Core Skills Science, Grade 7

9. Vocabulary Describe the structure of the human body using the terms *cell*, *tissue*, *organ*, and *organ system*.

_____

_____

_____

_____

10. Reading Skill: Main Idea and Details Which cell organelle is responsible for producing most of the ATP within an organism?

_____

_____

11. Critical Thinking: Analyze What is the importance of having a cell's digestive enzymes enclosed inside lysosomes?

_____

_____

_____

12. Inquiry Skill: Use Models Draw a diagram to model a plant cell. Include a cell wall, chloroplasts, and a large central vacuole.

13. Test Prep Cell structures are important for the cell to function properly, and each cell structure is responsible for a different function. What can you infer about cells with cell walls?

  A They are unicellular organisms.

  B The cell walls help support the cell and the organism.

  C They obtain their nutrition by engulfing other organisms.

  D The cell walls capture energy from sunlight to make food.

© Houghton Mifflin Harcourt Publishing Company

How Do Plants Reproduce?

Kingdom Plantae

Plants are classified within the kingdom Plantae. Plants are organisms that have cell walls made of cellulose and that usually conduct photosynthesis. Most plants have a large number of chloroplasts, which contain the green pigment chlorophyll. This is why most plants are green.

Plants can be classified as vascular or nonvascular, based on whether they have vascular tissue, which is used to transport nutrients and water. Plants can also be classified based on whether or not they produce seeds. For seeded plants, the seed is either encased in an ovule or fruit (angiosperms) or the seed is unenclosed or bare (gymnosperms). Plants, like other organisms, reproduce, passing on their genetic information and maintaining the population levels of their species. In general, reproduction occurs when one or more parent organism produces offspring. There are two main types of reproduction, asexual reproduction and sexual reproduction, and plants use both types.

Asexual Reproduction in Plants

Asexual reproduction involves only one parent organism and does not involve sex cells, or gametes. Since only one parent is involved in asexual reproduction, the offspring are genetically identical to the parent.

Asexual reproduction in plants can take many forms. Non-specialized parts of the plant can fragment from the parent organism. This plant fragment may be able to regenerate and form a new plant that is genetically identical to the parent. Examples of plants that reproduce through fragmentation and regeneration are mosses and liverworts. Gardeners often take advantage of fragmentation and regeneration in plants. Whenever a new plant is grown from cuttings of a parent plant, humans are using asexual reproduction in plants.

Asexual reproduction in plants can also occur through more specialized reproductive structures, such as spores, or through vegetative reproductive structures, such as runners, plantlets, or tubers. Runners, or stolons, are roots that spread just below the ground. Genetically identical offspring can form from buds on a stolon. In a similar manner, some plants develop plantlets, or small plants, at the end of stolons as a means of asexual reproduction. Tubers are enlarged sections of a plant that are used to store nutrients. Some plants also use tubers for asexual reproduction. Potatoes are an example of tubers.

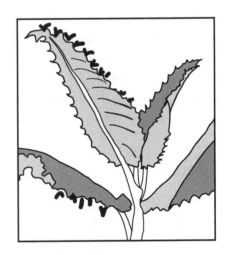

Kalanchoe plants produce **plantlets** along the edges of their leaves. The plantlets eventually fall off and root in the soil to grow into plants that form their own plantlets.

© Houghton Mifflin Harcourt Publishing Company

Alternation of Generations

Sexual reproduction involves the union of sex cells from two parents. The genetic material from both parents is combined in the offspring. Plants, algae, and some protists have a life cycle that regularly alternates between a haploid phase and a diploid phase. A haploid cell contains only one set of chromosomes and a diploid cell contains two set of chromosomes. Sex cells are typically haploid and body cells, or somatic cells, are typically diploid.

In plants, the diploid phase in the life cycle that produces spores is called a sporophyte. Specialized cells in the sporophyte produce spores. A spore is a haploid reproductive cell produced by meiosis that is capable of developing into an adult without fusing with another cell. Thus, unlike a gamete, a spore gives rise to a multicellular individual called a gametophyte without joining with another cell.

The gametophyte is the haploid phase that produces gametes. The gametophyte produces gametes that combine during sexual reproduction and give rise to the diploid phase. Thus, the sporophyte and gametophyte generations take turns, or alternate, in the life cycle.

Flowers

Angiosperms are flowering plants that produce seeds within an ovary or fruit. A flower is a reproductive structure formed by angiosperm sporophytes. A flower consists of a few basic parts: the sepals, the petals, the stamens, and the carpels.

The stamens are the male reproductive organs and the carpels are the female reproductive organs. A stamen is made up of an anther attached to a filament stalk. Male gametophytes form as pollen grains within the anther. A carpel is made up of a small structure called a stigma attached to a narrow stalk called the style. At the base of a carpel is an ovary where female gametophytes form as embryo sacs.

Pollination occurs when pollen is transferred from an anther to a stigma. Pollination can occur between the reproductive structures of the same plant or between different plants. Pollen can be transferred by wind or by animals. In fact, many plants have evolved mutualistic relationships with animal pollinators. The animals, such as insects or birds, receive nectar from the flower, and the plants benefit from increased pollination. During pollination, the pollen grain lands on the stigma and travels down the style to fertilize the embryo sac. The embryo then develops into a seed.

Seeds

Some plants reproduce through seeds. A seed is a structure that contains the embryo of a plant. An embryo is an early stage in the development of plants and animals. Most plants living today are seed plants—vascular plants that produce seeds. Some, such as pine trees, are gymnosperms, seed plants whose seeds do not develop within a sealed container (a fruit). Most seed plants are flowering plants, or angiosperms. Angiosperms produce seeds that develop enclosed within a specialized structure called a fruit.

© Houghton Mifflin Harcourt Publishing Company

How Do Plants Reproduce?

Match each definition to its term.

Definitions   **Terms**

_____ **1.** female reproductive organ in plants   **a.** seed

_____ **2.** male reproductive organ in plants   **b.** diploid

_____ **3.** structure containing embryo of a plant   **c.** haploid

_____ **4.** reproductive structure formed by angiosperms   **d.** stamen

_____ **5.** transfer of pollen from an anther to a stigma   **e.** flower

_____ **6.** cell with one set of chromosomes   **f.** carpel

_____ **7.** cell with two sets of chromosomes   **g.** pollination

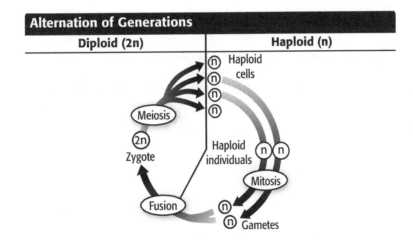

8. Main Idea How do plants use both sexual and asexual reproduction?

_____

_____

_____

_____

7

9. **Vocabulary** Explain alternation of generations using the terms *gametophyte*, *sporophyte*, *diploid*, and *haploid*.

_____

_____

_____

_____

10. **Reading Skill: Cause and Effect** What happens when pollen is transferred from an anther to a stigma?

_____

_____

11. **Critical Thinking: Evaluate** Explain one advantage and one disadvantage of asexual reproduction in plants.

_____

_____

_____

12. **Inquiry Skill: Apply** Why are pollinators important to plants and to humans?

_____

_____

_____

13. **Test Prep** Which statement accurately describes the alternation of generations in plants?

  A one life cycle for male plants and a different life cycle for female plants

  B a life cycle in which haploid gametophytes alternate with diploid sporophytes

  C two life cycles during which either sexual or asexual reproduction takes place

  D a life cycle in which fertilization alternates with mitosis

© Houghton Mifflin Harcourt Publishing Company

How Does Photosynthesis Cycle Matter and Energy?

Photosynthesis

Almost all the energy used by living organisms is originally captured from sunlight. Plants, algae, and some bacteria capture this solar energy and use it to make complex molecules in a process called photosynthesis. These molecules serve as the source of energy, or food, for other organisms.

Photosynthesis occurs in the chloroplasts of plant cells and algae and in the cell membrane of certain prokaryotes. Chloroplasts are specialized organelles that have two membranes and their own DNA. Chloroplasts are green because they contain chlorophyll, a green pigment. Chlorophyll is found in an internal membrane system within a chloroplast. Chlorophyll traps the energy of sunlight. This energy is then used to make sugar.

Stages of Photosynthesis

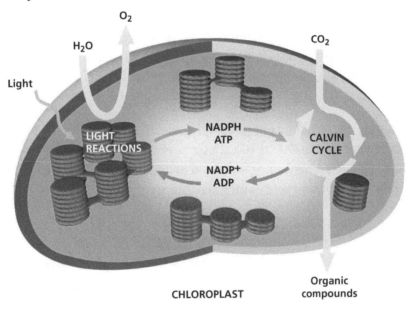

Photosynthesis has three stages. During stage 1, energy is captured from sunlight. Pigments in the chloroplasts, such as chlorophyll, absorb light, which excites electrons.

During stage 2, light energy is converted to chemical energy. The chemical energy is temporarily stored in the energy carrier molecules (ATP) and (NADPH). This stage occurs when the excited electrons are passed through a series of molecules – called an electron transport chain – along a structure called the thylakoid membrane.

During stage 3, the chemical energy stored in ATP and NADPH powers the formation of organic compounds using carbon dioxide and water. The most common way that this happens is called the Calvin cycle. The Calvin cycle uses ATP, NADPH, and a key enzyme to add carbon dioxide molecules to exiting carbon chains, which are used as the building blocks of sugars. The enzyme is regenerated at the end of the Calvin cycle, and the process begins again. The sugars produced during photosynthesis are either used immediately or stored for future use.

© Houghton Mifflin Harcourt Publishing Company

Life Science
Core Skills Science, Grade 7

Photosynthesis Supplies Energy and Oxygen

Photosynthesis is the process by which cells, such as plant cells, use sunlight, carbon dioxide, and water to make sugar and oxygen. Photosynthesis provides energy for almost all life forms. Photosynthesis can be summarized by the following equation:

Photosynthesis

$$6CO_2 + 6H_2O + \text{Light energy} \rightarrow C_6H_{12}O_6 + 6O_2$$

Carbon dioxide Water   Glucose   Oxygen

Photosynthesis supplies energy and oxygen because they are products of the chemical reactions that take place. Photosynthesis also requires reactants for the chemical reactions. These reactants, carbon dioxide and water, are products of a different process known as cellular respiration.

Cellular Respiration

Photosynthesis and cellular respiration are the interrelated processes by which living things capture, transform, and store energy. Photosynthesis is the process by which energy from sunlight is captured and transformed into chemical energy. Cellular respiration is the process cells use to harvest the energy in organic compounds.

Carbon dioxide and water are two reactants of photosynthesis that are products of cellular respiration. Similarly, sugar and oxygen are two reactants of cellular respiration that are products of photosynthesis. So, the two processes rely on each other to provide the reactants for each chemical reaction. In this way, photosynthesis and cellular respiration cycle matter and energy in living systems.

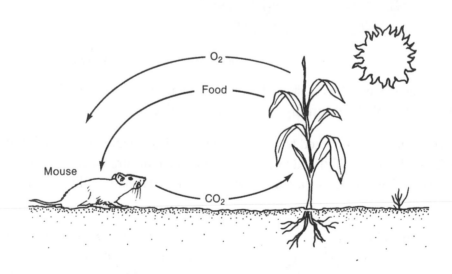

© Houghton Mifflin Harcourt Publishing Company

Name _____ Date _____

How Does Photosynthesis Cycle Matter and Energy?

Fill in the blanks.

Write the answer to the question on the lines below.

1. The process of _____ captures energy from the sun and uses it to produce sugar and oxygen from carbon dioxide and water.

2. Photosynthesis occurs in the _____ of plant cells.

3. Chlorophyll is a _____ that captures light.

4. The _____ is used to pass excited electrons in the thylakoid membrane.

5. Carbon dioxide and water are _____ in the process of photosynthesis.

6. Photosynthesis helps cycle _____ and _____ in living systems.

7. **Vocabulary** Write a short paragraph about photosynthesis using the terms *plant*, *chloroplast*, *chlorophyll*, *pigment*, *sugar*, *oxygen*, and *sunlight*.

_____

_____

_____

_____

_____

_____

_____

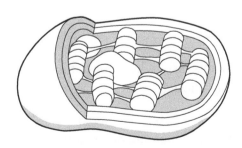

Chloroplast

© Houghton Mifflin Harcourt Publishing Company

8. Main Idea Identify the substances that are needed for photosynthesis and the substances that are produced by photosynthesis.

_____

_____

_____

9. Reading Skill: Analyze Animal cells do not contain chloroplasts. What does this indicate about how animals must get the sugars they need to produce chemical energy that their cells can use?

_____

_____

_____

10. Inquiry Skill: Infer Phaedra conducted an experimental investigation of the gas production of a water plant. She placed a beaker upside down over a water plant submerged in water and collected the gas that the water plant produced when kept in sunlight. After several days, a large bubble of gas collected in the upside-down beaker, as shown below.

Given that the gas came from the water plant, what is the content of the bubble of gas collected in the test tube? What process produced this gas?

_____

_____

11. Test Prep Autotrophs, such as plants, use light to make their own food. What happens to the light absorbed by a plant during photosynthesis?

   A It is converted to kinetic energy.

   B It is converted to chemical energy, which the plant stores.

   C It powers a reaction that produces carbon dioxide and water.

   D It powers a reaction that produces oxygen and carbon dioxide.

© Houghton Mifflin Harcourt Publishing Company

How Do Humans Respond to Stimuli?

Have you ever jumped at a loud sound or pulled your hand away from a hot object? In both instances, your body is gathering information from the environment, processing the information, and causing a response. Animals have developed the nervous system in order to respond to stimuli from both their external environments and their internal conditions. A stimulus is anything that elicits a response from an organism.

Sensory Receptors

Nerves are part of the nervous system. In the human body, the nervous system is made up of the brain, spinal cord, nerves, and sensory organs. The nervous system is responsible for regulating behavior, maintaining homeostasis, regulating other organ systems, and controlling sensory and motor functions.

Humans have five sensory organs. The nose is used to smell. The ears are used to hear. The eyes are used to see. The mouth is used to taste. And, the skin is used to feel. These organs include nervous tissue and are used to gather stimuli from the external environment.

Nervous tissue consists of nerve cells, or neurons, and their supporting cells. A neuron's unique branching structure enables it to conduct electrical signals called nerve impulses. Dendrites extend from the cell body of the neuron and are the "antennae" of the neuron. An axon is a long membrane-covered extension of the cytoplasm that conducts nerve impulses. The cells of nerve tissue are specialized to conduct signals.

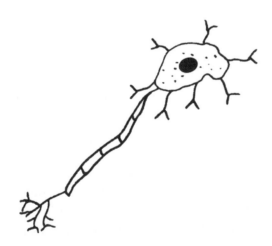

Different nerve cells respond to different stimuli. Eyes have photoreceptors that can detect light. Nerve cells in the ears are capable of detecting sound waves, which are a type of mechanical wave. The sense of smell and the sense of taste are based on nerve cells that can detect chemical stimuli.

© Houghton Mifflin Harcourt Publishing Company

Information Processing

Neurons are connected throughout the human body. When a stimulus is detected, the nerve signal is passed along neurons until it reaches the central nervous system. The brain is part of the central nervous system, and the brain is responsible for processing information collected by the sensory organs. The brain is extremely complex and capable of almost instantaneous decision making based on memories and the current environment. The human brain processes stimuli continuously. As the information is processed, the brain may send signals back to the body that cause a response.

Response to Stimuli

If nerves in your hand are exposed to extreme temperatures by getting too close to a hot iron, the signal is passed to the brain. The brain processes the information and sends a signal back to the hand. In this case, the hand may be jerked away quickly in a reflexive reaction that occurs almost as quickly as the hot object is encountered. Reflexes such as these are adaptations that help prevent extreme damage.

Stimuli do not always cause reflexive reactions. The brain may send a signal to the body that causes a slower reaction. For example, if you walk outside in the morning and the photoreceptors in your eyes sense that the sun is too bright, your brain might process the information and send a signal that makes you squint and then put on your sunglasses.

Stimuli can also cause memories to be stored in the brain. You remember certain smells or sounds. This is because your brain can process sensory inputs, store the information as memories, and cause an immediate behavioral reaction.

Homeostasis

All living organisms must maintain a stable internal environment in order to function properly. The maintenance of stable internal conditions in spite of changes in the external environment is called homeostasis. The body maintains homeostasis by sensing and responding to changes in the external environment.

Almost all body processes use a system called negative feedback to maintain homeostasis. Negative feedback is a system in which the results of a process provide a signal for the process to stop. One example of this is the regulation of body temperature. Despite temperature changes in the environment, our bodies maintain a fairly constant internal temperature of about 37 °C. The body regulates its internal temperature using negative feedback in much the same way that a thermostat works. When the body senses that its internal temperature has dropped below normal, a chemical signal causes the body to shiver, which results in heat. When your body temperature returns to normal, the chemical signal is turned off, and you stop shivering. If your body temperature rises above normal, another chemical signal is sent. This signal tells the body to begin cooling itself through the evaporation of sweat and by increasing blood flow to small vessels below the skin. This releases heat and cools the body. This is important because if temperatures become too high, proteins begin to denature (change shape) and stop functioning. If temperatures drop too far below the normal range, cellular processes will stop.

© Houghton Mifflin Harcourt Publishing Company

How Do Humans Respond to Stimuli?

Fill in the blanks

1. _____ is the maintenance of a stable internal environment.

2. A(n) _____ is anything that elicits a response from an organism.

3. The body uses a _____ system to maintain homeostasis.

4. Eyes have _____ that can detect light.

5. The _____ is responsible for regulating behavior, maintaining homeostasis, and controlling sensory and motor functions.

6. A(n) _____ is a long membrane-covered extension of the cytoplasm that conducts nerve impulses.

7. _____ is a response to provide heat for the body.

8. **Main Idea** Explain how humans respond to stimuli.

_____

_____

_____

_____

© Houghton Mifflin Harcourt Publishing Company

Life Science
Core Skills Science, Grade 7

9. Vocabulary Write a paragraph describing how the human body gathers, processes, and responds to information from the environment or internal conditions. Use the terms *nerve* and *stimulus*.

_____

_____

_____

10. Reading Skill: Compare and Contrast How are nerve cells in the eyes different from nerve cells in the ears?

_____

_____

_____

11. Critical Thinking: Analyze Why is it important for the brain to process information quickly and accurately?

_____

_____

_____

12. Inquiry Skill: Observe How does your body respond to these stimuli: a favorite smell and a dark room?

_____

_____

_____

13. Test Prep Which of the following describes how the human body would react to a high external temperature to maintain homeostasis?

A The body will shiver to lower its internal temperature.

B The body will sweat to lower its internal temperature.

C The body will shiver to raise its internal temperature.

D The body will sweat to raise its internal temperature.

© Houghton Mifflin Harcourt Publishing Company

What Are Food Webs?

Food Chains

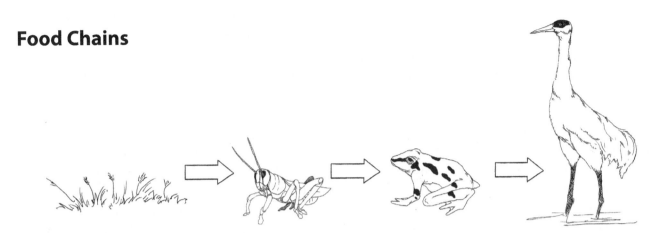

All living things are connected in the web of life. Energy and other resources flow between living organisms and their environment. The living components of an ecosystem are known as the biotic factors and the nonliving components of an ecosystem are known as the abiotic factors. Ecologists study how energy moves through an ecosystem by assigning organisms in that ecosystem to a specific level, called a trophic level, based on the organism's source of energy. Energy moves from one trophic level to another.

A diagram that shows the path of energy through the trophic levels of an ecosystem is called a food chain. The arrow in a food chain shows the direction of matter and energy flow. That is, each arrow points to the organism that consumes the other organism as food.

Food Webs

Because few organisms eat only one kind of food, the energy connections in nature are more accurately shown by a food web than by a food chain. A food web is a diagram that shows the feeding relationships between organisms in an ecosystem.

Notice in the food web to the right that an arrow goes from the prairie dog to the coyote. This arrow indicates that the coyote consumes, or eats, the prairie dog. The coyote needs the prairie dog's matter and energy in order to survive. The mountain lion also consumes the prairie dog. Matter and energy move from one organism to the next in one direction in a food web. The arrows show the direction of this movement. Each organism uses that matter and energy for its life processes.

© Houghton Mifflin Harcourt Publishing Company

Life Science
Core Skills Science, Grade 7

Classifying Organisms

Organisms that change the energy in sunlight into chemical energy or food are called producers. Producers do this through the process of photosynthesis. Most producers are green plants, but algae and some bacteria are also producers. The lowest trophic level of any ecosystem is occupied by the producers. Grasses are the main producers in the prairie ecosystem. Examples of producers in other ecosystems include cordgrass and algae in a salt marsh and trees in a forest.

Not all organisms can make their own food like producers can. Some organisms must eat other organisms to obtain energy and nutrients. These organisms are called consumers. There are several kinds of consumers. A consumer that eats only plants is called an herbivore. Examples include grasshoppers and bison. A consumer that eats other animals is called a carnivore. Badgers and owls are carnivores. Consumers that eat both plants and animals are called omnivores. The grasshopper mouse is an omnivore that eats insects and grass seeds. Herbivores are considered primary consumers, and so they occupy the second trophic level of an ecosystem. Carnivores are considered secondary consumers, since they eat animals that have already fed on plants. Carnivores are part of the third trophic level in ecosystems. Some ecosystems have a fourth trophic level composed of carnivores that consume other carnivores. These carnivores are known as tertiary consumers.

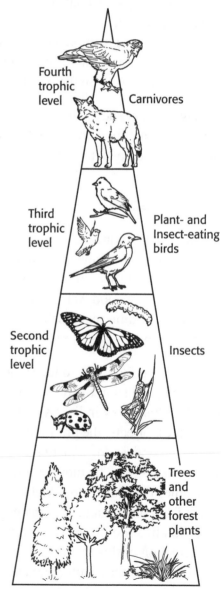

Fourth trophic level — Carnivores

Third trophic level — Plant- and Insect-eating birds

Second trophic level — Insects

Trees and other forest plants

First trophic level

Scavengers are also omnivores. A scavenger is an animal that feeds on dead plants and animals that it finds in its environment. The turkey vulture is a scavenger in the prairie. A vulture will eat what is left after a coyote has killed and eaten part of an animal. Scavengers also eat animals and plants that have died from natural causes.

Organisms that get energy and nutrients by breaking down dead organisms are called decomposers. Bacteria and fungi are decomposers. Decomposers produce simple materials such as water and carbon dioxide that can be used by other organisms. Decomposers are nature's recyclers because they return valuable nutrients to the soil or water.

© Houghton Mifflin Harcourt Publishing Company

What Are Food Webs?

Write answers to the questions on the lines below.

1. What is a scavenger?

_____

2. What is a decomposer?

_____

3. What is a producer?

_____

4. What is a consumer?

_____

5. What does an arrow show in a food chain or food web?

_____

6. Main Idea How are food chains and food webs alike, and how are they different?

_____

_____

_____

_____

Food Web Diagram

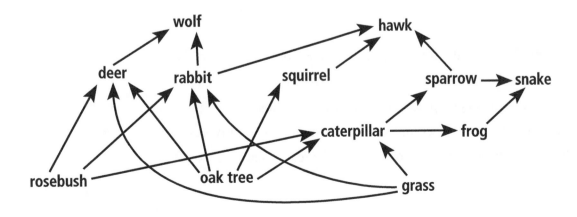

© Houghton Mifflin Harcourt Publishing Company

Life Science
Core Skills Science, Grade 7

7. Vocabulary Write a short paragraph using the terms *omnivore*, *carnivore*, and *herbivore*.

_____

_____

_____

8. Reading Skill: Main Idea and Details Why are decomposers known as "nature's recyclers?"

_____

_____

_____

9. Critical Thinking: Synthesize Explain why scavengers and decomposers are also consumers.

_____

_____

_____

_____

10. Inquiry Skill: Use Models Draw a diagram to model a food web from an ecosystem. Be sure to include producers, consumers, and decomposers, as well as arrows that show how matter and energy are transferred within the food web.

11. Test Prep Which of the following is the correct order in a food chain?

   A Sun → producers → scavengers → herbivores → carnivores

   B Sun → consumers → predators → parasites → hosts

   C Sun→ producers → decomposers → consumers → omnivores

   D Sun → producers → herbivores → carnivores → scavengers

© Houghton Mifflin Harcourt Publishing Company

What Is Meiosis?

Cell Division

There are two types of cell division: mitosis and meiosis. In mitosis, each nucleus ends up with the same number and kinds of chromosomes as the original cell. The new cells that form are identical to the original cell. Meiosis is a form of cell division that halves the number of chromosomes when forming specialized reproductive cells, such as gametes or spores. Meiosis involves two divisions of the nucleus—meiosis I and meiosis II.

Meiosis I

Before meiosis begins, during interphase, the DNA (deoxyribonucleic acid) in the original cell is replicated. DNA contains the genetic information of an organism, and DNA is organized into structures called chromosomes. Entire chromosomes are replicated at the beginning of meiosis, forming homologous chromosomes. Homologous chromosomes are similar in size, shape, and genetic content.

During prophase I, the chromosomes condense, and the nuclear envelope breaks down. Homologous chromosomes pair along their length. Crossing-over occurs when portions of one homologous chromosome are broken and exchanged with the corresponding portions of the other homologous chromosome. Crossing-over increases genetic diversity within a population.

During metaphase I, the pairs of homologous chromosomes are moved by the spindle to the middle of the cell. The homologous chromosomes remain together, but they are randomly or independently sorted. This is another mechanism that increases genetic diversity.

During anaphase I, the homologous chromosomes separate. As in mitosis, the chromosomes of each pair are pulled to opposite poles of the cell by the spindle fibers. But the chromatids do not separate yet—each chromosome is still composed of two chromatids. The genetic material, however, has recombined.

During telophase I, individual chromosomes gather at each of the poles. In most organisms, the cytoplasm divides, a process called cytokinesis, forming two new cells. Both cells or poles contain one chromosome from each pair of homologous chromosomes. Chromosomes do not replicate between meiosis I and meiosis II.

© Houghton Mifflin Harcourt Publishing Company

Meiosis II

During prophase II, a new spindle forms around the chromosomes. During metaphase II, the chromosomes line up along the equator and are attached at their centromeres to spindle fibers. During anaphase II, the centromeres divide, and the chromatids (now called chromosomes) move to opposite poles of the cell. During telophase II, a nuclear envelope forms around each set of chromosomes. The spindle breaks down, and the cell undergoes cytokinesis. The final result of meiosis is four haploid cells. The term haploid refers to a cell that has half the chromosome number as a regular body cell, which is considered a diploid cell. So, diploid cells have two sets of chromosomes, one from each parent, and haploid cells have one set of chromosomes.

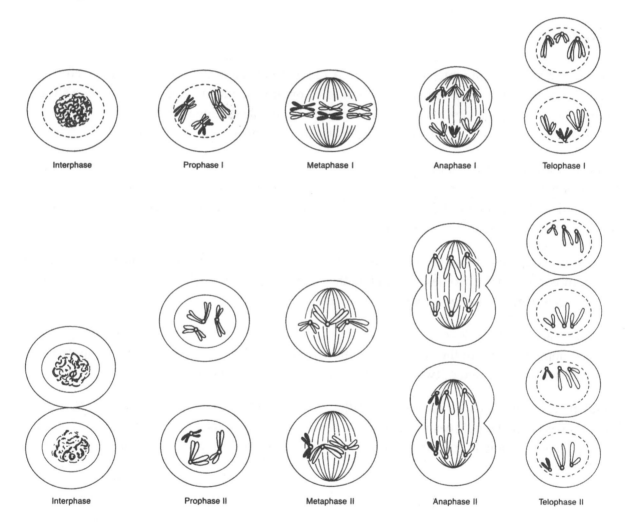

| Interphase | Prophase I | Metaphase I | Anaphase I | Telophase I |

| Interphase | Prophase II | Metaphase II | Anaphase II | Telophase II |

Sexual Reproduction

Some organisms reproduce by joining gametes to form the first cell of a new individual. The gametes are haploid – they contain one copy of each chromosome. The haploid gametes are formed through meiosis. A diploid mother and father give rise to haploid gametes, which join to form diploid offspring. Because both parents contribute genetic material, the offspring have traits of both parents but are not exactly like either parent. Sexual reproduction, with the formation of haploid cells, occurs in eukaryotic organisms, including humans. Sexual reproduction provides a powerful means of quickly making different combinations of genes among individuals.

© Houghton Mifflin Harcourt Publishing Company

What Is Meiosis?

Fill in the blanks.

1. DNA is organized into structures called _____, which are replicated at the beginning of meiosis I.

2. During a process called _____, the cytoplasm of a cell divides.

3. Humans reproduce through _____ reproduction.

4. Chromosomes that are similar in size, shape, and genetic content are _____ chromosomes.

5. A cell is considered _____ if it has one half the chromosome number as a regular body cell of that species.

6. Portions of homologous chromosomes can be exchanged in a process known as

   _____, which can increase genetic diversity.

7. _____ are specialized reproductive cells.

8. **Main Idea** Mitosis and meiosis are two types of cell division. Explain the major difference between mitosis and meiosis.

   _____

   _____

   _____

   _____

9. **Vocabulary** Write a sentence using the terms *meiosis* and *sexual reproduction*.

   _____

   _____

© Houghton Mifflin Harcourt Publishing Company

10. Reading Skill: Cause and Effect Explain two ways in which genetic diversity can be increased during meiosis.

_____

_____

_____

11. Critical Thinking: Analyze Imagine that sex cells resulted from mitosis instead of meiosis. What would then be the result of fertilization of an egg by a sperm cell? Explain.

_____

_____

_____

12. Inquiry Skill: Use Models Create a graphic organizer, such as a flow chart or concept map, that models meiosis. Include each stage name and a synopsis of what occurs during each stage. Use your own paper if needed.

13. Test Prep During metaphase II, homologous chromosomes line up next to each other. If one arm of a chromatid crosses over the arm of another chromatid, what results?

    A The creation of an additional sex cell

    B The independent assortment of genetic material

    C A possible change in the offspring cell's functionality

    D Additional variation in the DNA combination of each sex cell formed

© Houghton Mifflin Harcourt Publishing Company

How Are Fossils Evidence of Common Ancestry?

Fossils

A fossil is the preserved or mineralized remains or imprint of an organism that lived long ago. Organisms can become preserved through many different processes. Fossils can range from an imprint of an organism to the bones of an organism to the entire preserved organism. The type of fossil formed depends upon the composition of the organism and the environmental conditions in which it is being preserved. Many organisms were preserved when they were buried in sedimentary rock. Fossilization in this manner usually preserves only the hard parts of the organism, such as the bone or shell. Other ways organisms are fossilized include becoming trapped

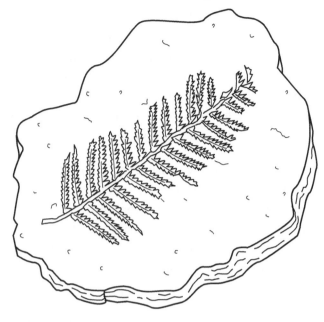

and preserved in resin from a tree, which becomes amber; becoming trapped and preserved in an asphalt pit (commonly called a tar pit); becoming frozen and preserved in cold climates; or becoming petrified through the mineralization of tissues. All fossils found on Earth are part of the fossil record, which contains information about the history of life on Earth.

Record of Evolution

Scientists estimate that the planet is 4.6 billion years old. From fossil evidence, scientists know that Earth and its living things have changed a great deal during its history. They know that the kinds of fossils found in older rock layers are different from the fossils found in newer rock. They can arrange fossils according to their age to build evidence of the gradual and orderly change of Earth's populations. This gradual and orderly change in populations is called evolution, and fossils are the most direct evidence to support the theory of evolution.

Modern evolutionary theory began in 1859 when Charles Darwin presented convincing evidence that species and populations evolve and proposed an explanation of how evolution happens. Darwin proposed that individuals that have traits better suited to their environment are more likely to survive and will reproduce more successfully than those that do not have those traits. In time, he said, the number of individuals that carry favorable traits that are inherited will increase in a population.

Darwin used fossil evidence to predict that intermediate forms between great groups of organisms would eventually be found. Indeed, many fossils have been discovered that demonstrate transitions between major groups. Today, Darwin's theory of evolution by natural selection is accepted by scientists as the best explanation of the biological diversity on Earth. Based on a large body of supporting evidence, scientists who study the early Earth agree on the following:

- Earth is about 4.6 billion years old.
- Organisms have lived on Earth for most of its history.
- All organisms living today share common ancestry with earlier, simpler life forms.

© Houghton Mifflin Harcourt Publishing Company

Fossil Evidence of Common Ancestry

Scientists can study the fossils they find to see if they have similarities to organisms alive today or to organisms that they know lived in the past. They can use the similarities to make inferences about the organism that formed the fossil. For example, if scientists are lucky, the remains of the entire organism will be present. In that case, the scientists can easily reconstruct what the organism looked like. More often, though, only partial remains are present, and the scientists must reconstruct the organism from fossil bits, such as a few bones or a shell. Then scientists must use what they already know to make an informed inference about how the pieces of the fossil fit together and what the pieces tell them.

Lines of evolutionary descent and common ancestry can be inferred by studying the anatomy and development of organisms living today and organisms present in the fossil record. Comparisons of the anatomy of different kinds of organism often show basic similarities, even when the structures' functions differ. For example, the similarities of structures in different vertebrates provide evidence that all vertebrates share a common ancestor. The forelimbs of vertebrates contain the same kinds of bones, which form in the same way during embryological development. These structures that share common ancestry are known as homologous structures.

Scientists can use further similarities between fossils and present-day organisms to infer additional characteristics of the fossil organism, such as what it ate, what ate it, and how it reproduced. The information that scientists gather about a fossil organism, in turn, can help them classify the organism based on evolutionary relationships. Scientists use information about species to sketch out a "tree of life" that includes all known organisms. Scientists know that their information is incomplete. For example, parts of Earth's history lack a fossil record. In fact, fossils are rare because specific conditions are necessary for fossils to form.

Other Evidence of Common Ancestry

In a similar way, a history of common ancestry can be found in the embryonic development of organisms. At some time in their embryonic development, all vertebrates have a tail, buds that become limbs, and pharyngeal pouches. Only adult fish and immature amphibians retain their pharyngeal pouches after birth.

Biological molecules also show evolutionary relationships. A comparison of DNA or amino-acid sequences shows that some species are more genetically similar than others. Differences in amino acid sequences and DNA sequences are greater between species that are more distantly related than between species that are closely related. These comparisons, like those in anatomy, are evidence of hereditary relationships among the species.

© Houghton Mifflin Harcourt Publishing Company

How Are Fossils Evidence of Common Ancestry?

Fill in the blanks.

1. The fossil _____ consists of all fossils found on Earth.

2. Scientists estimate that Earth is about _____ years old.

3. Structures that share common ancestry are known as _____ structures.

4. A _____ is the preserved or mineralized remains or imprint of an organism that lived long ago.

5. Modern evolutionary theory began when _____ presented his theory of evolution through natural selection in 1859.

6. Organisms can become petrified through the _____ of tissues.

7. Scientists sketch out a _____ that contains all known organisms.

8. **Main Idea** What three lines of evidence can be used to infer common ancestry in organisms?

   _____

   _____

   _____

   _____

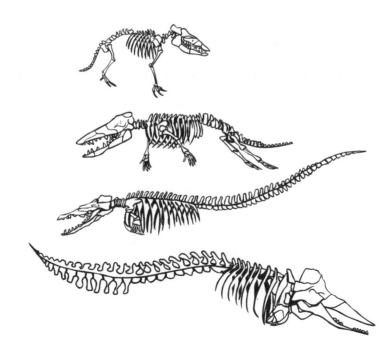

9. **Vocabulary** Write a paragraph describing five ways in which an organism can become fossilized. Use the terms *fossil* and *fossil record*.

_____

_____

_____

_____

10. **Reading Skill: Details** Why are fossils rare?

_____

_____

11. **Critical Thinking: Synthesize** How does the rarity of fossils impact the fossil record?

_____

_____

_____

12. **Inquiry Skill: Evaluate** How could you evaluate a fossil to determine possible lines of evolutionary descent?

_____

_____

_____

13. **Test Prep** Which of the following is **NOT** a condition that would lead to fossilization?

    A frozen in cold climate

    B preserved in tree resin

    C unburied on igneous rock

    D buried in sedimentary rock

© Houghton Mifflin Harcourt Publishing Company

What Is Artificial Selection?

Natural Selection

Have you ever thought about the diversity of life on Earth? The origins of the wide variety of plants, animals, fungi, and microorganisms on Earth can be traced back to the beginning of life by studying evolution. Evolution is the gradual change of populations over time. The idea of evolution through natural selection was developed by Charles Darwin. The heart of Darwin's theory of evolution is that natural selection is the mechanism by which adaptations develop and evolution occurs. The process of natural selection is defined by four important points that are true for all real populations.

First, all populations have genetic variation. That is, in any population there is an array of individuals that differ slightly from one another in genetic makeup. While this may be obvious in humans, it is also true in species whose members may appear identical, such as a species of bacteria.

Second, the environment presents challenges to successful reproduction. Naturally, an organism that does not survive to reproduce or whose offspring die before reproducing does not pass on its genes to future generations.

Third, individuals tend to produce more offspring than the environment can support. Thus, individuals of a population often compete with one another to survive.

Finally, individuals that are better able to cope with the challenges presented by their environment tend to leave more offspring than those individuals less suited to the environment.

Artificial Selection

Artificial selection is a term first used by Darwin to explain his theory of evolution through natural selection. Artificial selection works in the same manner as natural selection, only humans, instead of nature, are applying the selective pressure. Farmers and breeders have been practicing artificial selection for centuries by selectively breeding certain plants and animals based on desired characteristics. For this reason, artificial selection is also known as selective breeding.

Take dogs for example. All dogs belong to the same subspecies, Canis lupis familiaris. However, some dogs are very different. Can you imagine a large dog, such as a Great Dane, and a small dog, such as a Chihuahua, standing side by side? It is hard to imagine that they are the same species of animal. The large variety in the dog species is not due to selective pressures from their environment, such as the need for a certain coat color or the advantage of a certain stature. Instead, the variety is due to human breeders' selectively breeding certain individuals to increase desirable traits in the population. For example, Great Danes were originally bred to hunt deer and wild boar, so human breeders selected large, well-muscled dogs to breed. Chihuahuas, on the other hand, were breed to be companion animals, so smaller individuals were chosen to breed.

Today, scientists use the principles set forth by Gregor Johann Mendel to create better crops and animals. They use the fundamentals of genetics to produce crops that have favorable traits, such as better yields and better flavor and that are most pest-resistant. By applying what they know about how traits are passed from generation to generation, scientists can produce organisms that help meet human needs.

© Houghton Mifflin Harcourt Publishing Company

Artificial Selection and Modern Genetics

Modern genetics is based on Gregor Johann Mendel's explanations for the patterns of heredity that he studied in garden pea plants. Before the experiments of Mendel in the mid-1800s, many people thought offspring were a blend of the traits of their parents. They thought that if a tall plant were crossed with a short plant, the offspring would be medium in height. Mendel's first experiments used monohybrid crosses (crosses between individuals that involve one pair of contrasting traits). For example, crossing a plant with purple flowers and a plant with white flowers is a monohybrid cross. Mendel's first experiments were carried out in three steps.

First, Mendel produced a true-breeding parental (P) generation. Then, he produced a first (FI) generation through cross-pollination of the P generation. All individuals from the F1 generation displayed the dominant trait from the P generation. The second (F2) generation was produced by allowing the F1 generation to self-pollinate. In the F2 generation, three individuals displayed the dominant trait for every one that displayed the recessive trait (a 3-to-1 ratio).

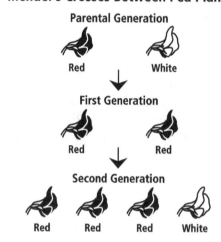

Mendel's Crosses Between Pea Plants

Mendel carefully studied seven characteristics of pea plants. He determined that alleles, or alternative forms of genes, govern the characteristics of organisms, such as the flower color in pea plants. For each of the seven characteristics that Mendel studied in this experiment, he found a similar 3-to-1 ratio of contrasting dominant to recessive traits in the second generation. Mendel's experiments showed that a combination of alleles determine traits. The set of alleles that an individual has for a characteristic is called the genotype. The trait that results from a set of alleles is the phenotype. In other words, genotype determines phenotype. Phenotype can also be affected by conditions in the environment, such as nutrients and temperature. If an individual has two of the same allele of a certain gene, the individual is homozygous for the related character. On the other hand, if an individual has two different alleles of a certain gene, the individual is heterozygous for the related character. In the heterozygous case, the dominant allele is expressed.

Although Mendel was correct about the inheritance of the traits he studied, scientists have learned that most patterns of inheritance are more complex than those that Mendel identified. Geneticists continue to study the inheritance of traits and to increase the manner in which artificial selection can be used to solve human problems.

© Houghton Mifflin Harcourt Publishing Company

What Is Artificial Selection?

Fill in the blanks.

1. A _____ cross is a cross between individuals that involves one pair of contrasting traits.

2. Artificial selection is also known as _____.

3. _____ is the gradual change of populations over time.

4. _____ and _____ have been practicing artificial selection for centuries.

5. The _____ is the set of alleles that an individual has for a characteristic.

6. All populations have _____ variation.

7. Alternative forms of genes are known as _____.

8. **Main Idea** What is artificial selection?

   _____

   _____

   _____

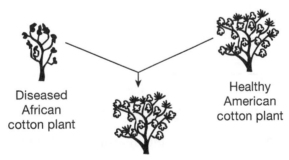

Diseased African cotton plant

Healthy American cotton plant

Healthy cotton plant produced to grow in Africa

© Houghton Mifflin Harcourt Publishing Company

9. **Vocabulary** Write a paragraph describing artificial selection using the terms *natural selection* and *genetics*.

_____

_____

_____

10. **Reading Skill: Compare and Contrast** Explain the difference between genotype and phenotype.

_____

_____

_____

11. **Critical Thinking: Evaluate** Why is genetic variation a key component of natural selection and artificial selection?

_____

_____

_____

12. **Inquiry Skill: Hypothesize** How could artificial selection be used to develop a new plant that is resistant to a certain pest?

_____

_____

_____

13. **Test Prep** Which of the following is an example of artificial selection?

   A The wide variety of birds

   B The wide variety of trees

   C The wide variety of dog breeds

   D The wide variety of bacteria

© Houghton Mifflin Harcourt Publishing Company

How Do Adaptations Help Organisms Survive?

Evolution through Natural Selection

Since life first appeared on Earth, many species have died out, and many new species have appeared. Through observing organisms found today and organisms found in the fossil record, scientists have discovered that species change over time. The process in which populations gradually change over time is called evolution.

Natural selection is an important part of evolution. Natural selection is the process by which organisms that are better adapted to their environment survive and reproduce more successfully than less well-adapted organisms. Populations of species can have a variety of different traits, or adaptations. Environmental factors determine which traits in a population are favorable. For example, the polar bear's white fur enables it to hunt successfully in its snowy environment. In a warmer environment, having white fur would not be an advantage. Favorable traits increase in a population as individuals with the adaptation experience greater reproductive success. Conversely, unfavorable traits decrease in a population as individuals with the trait experience limited reproductive success.

Adaptations

A characteristic that helps an organism survive and reproduce in its environment is called an adaptation. Adaptations may be physical, such as a long neck or striped fur. They may be biochemical factors, such as having proteins that can withstand very high temperatures. Adaptations might also be behaviors that help an organism find food, protect itself, or reproduce.

33

Examples of Adaptations

Plants and animals have adaptations that help them survive. Most birds can fly. Even flightless birds, such as ostriches, have ancestors that could fly. So, it is not surprising that birds have many adaptations for flight. The most obvious characteristic related to flight is the wings. But birds also have lightweight bodies, powerful flight muscles, and a rapidly beating heart. The fast heart helps birds get plenty of oxygen-rich blood to the flight muscles. The table below shows some adaptations of the beaks and feet of birds that live in different environments and eat different food.

Beak and Feet Adaptations			
Type of beak	Adapted for	Type of foot	Adapted for
	eating seeds		perching
	eating insects		wading
	probing for food		preying
	preying on animals		swimming
	straining food from water		climbing

Fishes have many adaptations that help them swim. Strong muscles attached to the backbone allow many fishes to swim quickly after their prey. To steer, stop, and balance, fishes use fins, which are fan-shaped structures that help fishes move. And many fishes have bodies covered by bony structures called scales. Scales protect the body and lower friction as fishes swim through the water. Fishes use their gills to breathe. A gill is an organ that removes oxygen from the water. Oxygen in the water passes through the thin membrane of the gills to the blood. The blood then carries oxygen through the body. Gills are also used to remove carbon dioxide from the blood.

Behaviors as Adaptations

Adaptations are not always physical characteristics. Some behaviors are also considered adaptations since they can help organisms survive and reproduce. From years of observation and experimentation, biologists have learned that many kinds of animal behaviors are influenced by genes. Genetically programmed behavior is often called innate behavior, or more commonly, instinct. The orb spider, for example, builds her web the same way every time. There is little or no variation in what she does, and her female offspring will build their webs in the same manner without being taught. This type of innate behavior is called fixed action pattern behavior because the action always occurs the same way.

© Houghton Mifflin Harcourt Publishing Company

How Do Adaptations Help Organisms Survive?

Write answers to the questions on the lines below.

1. What is a fixed action pattern behavior?

   _____

   _____

2. What is natural selection?

   _____

   _____

3. Why are adaptations important?

   _____

   _____

4. What is evolution?

   _____

5. How do gills help fishes survive?

   _____

   _____

6. What are instincts?

   _____

7. How do adaptations help organisms survive?

   _____

   _____

© Houghton Mifflin Harcourt Publishing Company

8. **Main Idea** Describe how adaptations, natural selection, and evolution are related.

_____

_____

_____

9. **Vocabulary** Write a paragraph explaining adaptations using the terms *survival*, *reproduction*, *environment*, and *behaviors*.

_____

_____

_____

10. **Reading Skill: Main Idea and Details** List some adaptations that help fishes swim.

_____

_____

11. **Critical Thinking: Synthesize** Why are some behaviors considered adaptations?

_____

_____

_____

12. **Inquiry Skill: Infer** Give an example of an unfavorable trait for a desert environment and a favorable trait for a desert environment. Which would be considered to be an adaptation?

_____

_____

_____

13. **Test Prep** Which of the following is the best example of a favorable adaptation to a snowy environment?

   A white fur

   B dark feathers

   C short beak

   D gills

© Houghton Mifflin Harcourt Publishing Company

What Is Biodiversity?

Biodiversity

Have you ever thought about all of the living things on Earth? Earth is covered by many different ecosystems, which are in turn populated by many different species. The variety of organisms, their genetic differences, and the communities and ecosystems in which they occur is termed biodiversity. Biodiversity is a measure of both the number of different species in a community, called species richness, and the relative numbers of each of the species, called species diversity.

The Importance of Biodiversity

Biodiversity is important to communities of organisms. So, how does biodiversity help the environment? Image a forest with only one kind of tree. If a disease were to hit that species, the entire forest might die. Now, imagine a forest with 10 species of trees. If a disease were to hit one species, 9 other species would remain. Bananas are an important crop. But banana fields are not very diverse. Fungi threaten the survival of bananas. Farmers often use chemicals to control fungi. Growing other plants among the bananas, or increasing biodiversity, can also prevent the spread of fungi. Experiments have clearly demonstrated that an ecosystem's biodiversity and productivity are related. That is, increased species richness leads to greater productivity.

Biodiversity is also important because each species has a unique role in an ecosystem. Losing one species could disrupt an entire ecosystem. For example, if an important predator is lost, its prey will multiply. The prey might eat more plants in an area, keeping other animals from getting food. Eventually, even the prey won't have food, so the prey will starve.

© Houghton Mifflin Harcourt Publishing Company

Biodiversity in Tropical Rainforests

Some of the most diverse communities are in tropical rainforests. Over the last 50 years, about half of the world's tropical rainforests have been burned to make pasture and farmland or have been cut for timber. Many thousands of square miles more are expected to be destroyed. The people and corporations responsible view the forest lands as a resource to be developed, much as Americans viewed North American forests a century ago.

The problem is that as the rainforests disappear, so do their inhabitants. Extinction occurs when a species no longer exists on Earth. No one knows how many species are becoming extinct. To find out, scientists carefully catalogue all of the residents of one small segment of forest and then extrapolate their data. That is, scientists use what they know to predict what they don't know. The resulting estimates vary widely, but it is clear that Earth is losing many species. Ten percent of well-known species teeter on the brink of extinction. Worst-case estimates are that we will lose up to one-fifth of the world's species of plants and animals—about one million species—during the next 50 years. An extinction of this size has not occurred in at least 65 million years, since the end of the age of dinosaurs.

A tragedy of extinction is that as species disappear, so do our chances to learn about them and their possible benefits. This situation is comparable to burning a library before reading the books—we lose forever the knowledge we might have gained.

Protecting Biodiversity

One way to maintain biodiversity is to protect individual species. In the United States, a law called the Endangered Species Act was designed to do just that. Endangered species are put on a special list. The law forbids activities that would harm a species on the list. The law also requires the development of recovery programs for each endangered species. Some endangered species, such as the California condor, are now increasing in number. Petitions are filed with the government to add a species to or remove a species from the endangered species list. The approval process can take years to complete. The government must study the species and its habitat before making a decision about whether the species should be considered endangered.

Waiting until a species is almost extinct to begin protecting it is like waiting until your teeth are rotting to begin brushing them. Scientists want to prevent species from becoming endangered and from becoming extinct. Plants, animals, and other microorganisms depend on one another. Each organism is part of a huge, interconnected web of organisms. The entire web should be protected to protect these organisms. To protect the web, complete habitats, not just individual species, must be preserved.

© Houghton Mifflin Harcourt Publishing Company

What Is Biodiversity?

Write the answers to the questions on the lines below.

1. What is extinction? _____

2. What is the Endangered Species Act? _____

   _____

3. Explain how the concept of biodiversity can help banana farmers?

   _____

   _____

4. Why is biodiversity important in ecosystems? _____

   _____

5. How are species richness and productivity related?

   _____

6. What is one way endangered species can be protected?

   _____

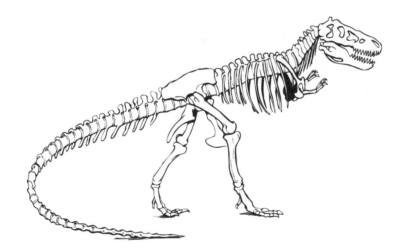

7. **Vocabulary** Write a definition for the term biodiversity that includes the terms *species richness* and *species diversity*.

   _____

   _____

   _____

© Houghton Mifflin Harcourt Publishing Company

Name _____ Date _____

8. Main Idea: Details Why are rain forests still being developed even though scientists understand the consequences of the loss of biodiversity?

_____

_____

9. Critical Thinking: Evaluate Imagine that a certain animal becomes extinct because of human activity. What effect, if any, would this have on the animal's prey and on its predators?

_____

_____

_____

10. Inquiry Skill: Observe Observe an ecosystem near your home or from a photo an adult helps you research. Describe the biodiversity of your chosen ecosystem.

_____

_____

_____

_____

_____

11. Test Prep Which human activity would most likely help maintain biodiversity in an area?

   A destruction of a major predator's habitat

   B introduction of a successful, competitive invasive species

   C use of pesticides, cleaning agents, and artificial fertilizers

   D introduction of laws to protect individual species

© Houghton Mifflin Harcourt Publishing Company

What Is the Universe?

The Universe

The universe is all of the matter and energy and space that exists. The universe consists of planets, solar systems, galaxies, nebulas, and all other parts of the cosmos. The universe is vast and constantly expanding. Astronomy is the field of science that deals with the formation, development, and composition of the entire universe. Astronomers study the parts of the universe and how the universe was formed.

Parts of the Universe

Earth is a planet in a solar system. A solar system includes a star and the objects that orbit it. Our solar system includes the sun, Earth, seven other planets, and many smaller objects such as moons, asteroids, and comets. About 99% of the mass in our solar system is made up of the sun. Earth and the other planets are small compared to the sun.

The sun is not close to any other stars in space. Most stars are bound to one or more stars by gravity. The smallest gravitationally bound star group is a binary system. It is made up of two stars that orbit each other. A multiple-star system includes more than two stars that orbit each other.

Some stars move through space together in a group bound by gravity. These stars make up a star cluster. Star clusters can be densely packed or loosely organized. Star clusters, binary systems, multiple-star systems, and solar systems are all found in galaxies. A galaxy is a large collection of stars, dust, and gas bound together by gravity. Our solar system resides in the Milky Way galaxy, which might have more than a trillion stars. It is about 100,000 light-years across. It takes the sun about 225 million years to orbit the center of the Milky Way.

Beyond the Milky Way galaxy, there are millions of other galaxies, each with billions of stars. Some of these galaxies form groups bound by gravity, just as stars do. The galactic group that includes the Milky Way is called the Local Group. The Local Group includes about 45 different galaxies of different shapes and sizes.

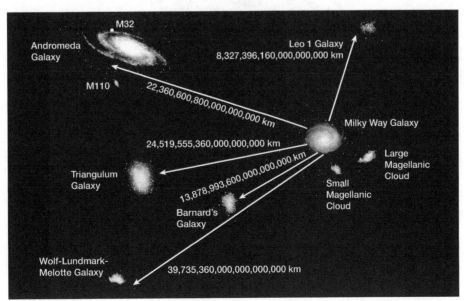

© Houghton Mifflin Harcourt Publishing Company

Formation of the Universe

The Big Bang theory is the widely accepted explanation for the formation of the universe. According to the theory, about 14 billion years ago, all matter and energy in the universe was compressed into an extremely small volume. An explosion of this matter and energy in all directions formed our expanding universe.

The Big Bang theory was first proposed because of observations of the Doppler effect of stars in distant galaxies. The Doppler effect is the apparent shift in the wavelength of a star toward or away from Earth. Astronomer Edwin Hubble observed that stars in distant galaxies had red shifts, meaning that they were moving away from our galaxy. He developed Hubble's law, which states that distant galaxies are moving away at speeds proportional to their distance from Earth. Hubble's law supports the idea of an expanding universe and the Big Bang theory.

Another facet of the Big Bang theory is that during the Big Bang, the universe would have been very hot and that as the universe expanded, it cooled. As the universe cooled, hydrogen and helium gases began to form. Scientists are not sure how the first galaxies and stars formed, but gravity may have caused small clouds of dust and gas to come together to form both. Alternatively, huge clumps of matter may have broken into smaller clouds of dust and gas. Scientists do know, however, that the force of gravity holds together the stars, dust, and gases that make up the countless galaxies in the universe.

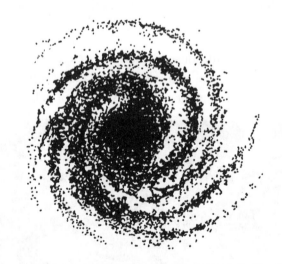

© Houghton Mifflin Harcourt Publishing Company

Earth Science
Core Skills Science, Grade 7

What Is the Universe?

Fill in the blanks.

1. Earth is part of the _____ galaxy.

2. The _____ theory explains how the universe formed from an explosion of matter and energy.

3. A(n) _____ is a collection of stars, dust, and gas bound together by gravity.

4. The _____ consists of all existing matter, energy, and space.

5. In a(n) _____ system, two stars orbit each other.

6. The _____ effect is an apparent shift in an observed wavelength.

7. A(n) _____ is a group of galaxies bound together by gravity.

8. **Main Idea** Describe the widely accepted explanation for the formation of the universe.

_____

_____

_____

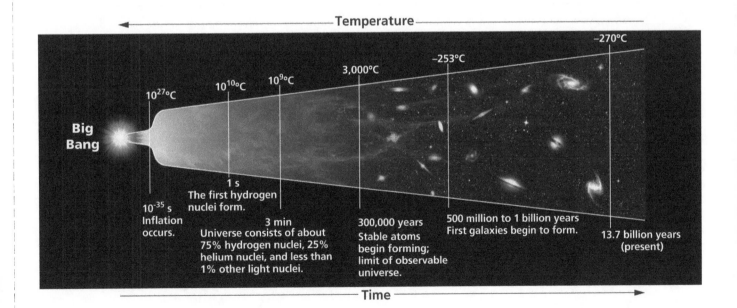

© Houghton Mifflin Harcourt Publishing Company

Earth Science
Core Skills Science, Grade 7

9. **Vocabulary** Describe the universe using the terms *planets*, *solar systems*, and *galaxies*.

_____

_____

_____

10. **Reading Skill: Main Idea and Details** How is the sun different from most other stars?

_____

_____

_____

11. **Critical Thinking: Evaluate** How is the Doppler effect used as evidence of an expanding universe?

_____

_____

_____

_____

12. **Inquiry Skill: Compare** Compare a binary system and a star cluster.

_____

_____

_____

13. **Test Prep** Which of the following correctly sequence objects in the universe from smallest to largest?

   A Local Group, solar system, Milky Way galaxy, Earth

   B Earth, Milky Way galaxy, solar system, Local Group

   C Earth, solar system, Milky Way galaxy, Local Group

   D Milky Way galaxy, Local Group, Earth, solar system

44

What Makes Up the Solar System?

Solar Systems

A solar system includes a star and the objects that orbit it. Gravity is the force that keeps objects in orbit around the central star, and sometimes around each other. Our solar system includes the sun, Earth, seven other planets, and many smaller objects such as moons, asteroids, and comets. About 99% of the mass in our solar system is made up of the sun. Earth and other planets are small compared to the sun.

Planets

A planet is a body in space that orbits a star, has cleared its orbit of debris, and has enough mass to obtain a round shape. There are eight planets in our solar system. Their order from closest to the sun is Mercury, Venus, Earth, Mars, Jupiter, Saturn, Uranus, and Neptune. The planets can be classified into two groups based on their characteristics. Terrestrial planets are relatively small and rocky. They include Mercury, Venus, Earth, and Mars. Gas giants are large and made mainly of light gases such as hydrogen and helium. They include Jupiter, Saturn, Uranus, and Neptune. Gas giants usually have rings and many moons. Moons are natural satellites that orbit a planet. Earth has one moon. Jupiter, the largest planet, has 62 known moons.

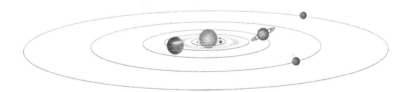

Other Objects in the Solar System

Other objects in the solar system include dwarf planets, asteroids, and comets. A dwarf planet is similar to a planet; however, unlike a planet, a dwarf planet has not cleared its orbit of debris. Pluto and Ceres are both dwarf planets. Some of the objects found near a dwarf planet include asteroids. An asteroid is a small, rocky object that orbits the sun. Asteroids often have irregular shapes. Tens of thousands of asteroids orbit between Mars and Jupiter in an area called the asteroid belt. Like asteroids, comets can have irregular shapes. A comet is a body of ice, rock, and gases that orbits the sun. When a comet nears the sun, some of its ice changes into glowing gases that form a long tail that may be visible from Earth.

© Houghton Mifflin Harcourt Publishing Company

Formation of the Solar System

Scientists have long debated the origins of the solar system. In 1796, the French mathematician Pierre-Simon Laplace made a hypothesis that is now known as the nebular hypothesis. It states that the sun and the planets condensed at about the same time out of a rotating cloud of gas and dust called a nebula.

Modern scientific calculations support Laplace's hypothesis and help explain how the sun and the planets formed from a nebula of gas and dust. The rotating cloud of dust and gas from which the sun and planets formed is called the solar nebula. Energy from collisions and pressure from gravity caused the center of the solar nebula to become hotter and denser. When the temperature at the center became high enough —about 10,000,000°C—hydrogen fusion began. A star formed, which is now called the sun. The sun is made up of about 99% of all the matter that was contained in the solar nebula.

While the sun was forming in the center of the solar nebula, planets were forming in the outer areas. Small bodies from which a planet originated are called planetesimals. Some planetesimals joined together through collisions and through the force of gravity to form larger bodies called protoplanets. The protoplanets' gravity attracted other planetesimals in the solar nebula. These planetesimals collided with the protoplanets and added their masses to the protoplanets. Eventually, the protoplanets became very large and dense, forming planets and moons.

So far, Earth is the only place that supports life as we know it. However, in the early 1990s, scientists discovered the first extra-solar planets orbiting distant stars. Today, more than 450 planets have been found orbiting 385 stars in other solar systems. Many of these planets are gas giants similar to Jupiter. None are like Earth. The search for an Earth-like planet continues.

© Houghton Mifflin Harcourt Publishing Company

What Makes Up the Solar System?

Write the answers to the questions on the lines below.

1. What is the nebular hypothesis?

   _____

   _____

2. Where would be the best place to search for asteroids in the solar system?

   _____

3. How does a dwarf planet differ from a planet?

   _____

   _____

4. What is a comet?

   _____

   _____

5. Where did most of the matter in the solar system end up after the solar system formed?

   _____

   _____

6. Name two dwarf planets.

   _____

7. What is a solar system?

   _____

8. What is a moon?

   _____

   _____

   _____

47

© Houghton Mifflin Harcourt Publishing Company

9. Main Idea What components make up a solar system?

_____

_____

10. Vocabulary Write a paragraph about the formation of planets using the terms *solar nebula*, *planetesimal*, *protoplanet*, and *planet*.

_____

_____

11. Reading Skill: Sequence List the planets in order from closest to the sun to farthest from the sun.

_____

_____

12. Critical Thinking: Synthesize Describe how gravity is important in a solar system.

_____

_____

_____

_____

13. Inquiry Skill: Use Models Draw a diagram that models a solar system. Be sure to include a star and other components of the solar system.

14. Test Prep Which of the following correctly describes the sequence in which Earth formed from the solar nebula?

   A planet → planetesimal → protoplanet

   B planetesimal → protoplanet → planet

   C protoplanet → planet → planetesimal

   D protoplanet → planetesimal → planet

© Houghton Mifflin Harcourt Publishing Company

What Is the Geologic Time Scale?

Fossil Record

Geology is the study of the formation, history, materials, and processes of the physical Earth. Geologists know that Earth changes over time. Changes to Earth can be slow and gradual, they can be fast and sudden, or they can be a mixture of both slow and gradual and fast and sudden.

One way scientists know that Earth has changed over time is by studying fossils and the fossil record. A fossil is the preserved remains of an organism. Organisms can become preserved in many ways, including preservation in amber, being buried in sedimentary rock, or becoming petrified. All of the fossils on Earth are part of the fossil record. The fossil record provides a history of life on Earth that can be studied and interpreted.

The Geologic Time Scale

The geologic time scale divides Earth's history into increasingly specific divisions. The broadest division is eons followed by eras, periods, epochs, and ages. The divisions are not a set length. Instead, scientists have created divisions based on large events in Earth's history that can be determined from the fossil record, such as mass extinctions or the rise of a particular group of organisms.

The four eons from oldest to youngest are the Hadean eon, the Archean eon, the Proterozoic eon, and the Phanerozoic eon. The Hadean, Archean, and Proterozoic eons can be further divided, but this lesson will focus on the Phanerozoic eon. The Phanerozoic eon can be divided into three eras. From oldest to youngest they are the Paleozoic era, the Mesozoic era, and the Cenozoic era.

The Paleozoic Era

The Paleozoic era is the oldest era in the Phanerozoic eon. The Paleozoic era can be divided into seven periods. The Cambrian period began around 543 million years ago. The Cambrian period is known for the "Cambrian explosion." Many of the modern animal groups evolved during this period. This includes shelled marine invertebrates and the first vertebrates.

The Ordovician period began 490 million years ago. During this period the atmosphere reached the current oxygen levels. During the Silurian period, which began 443 million years ago, land plants and animals first appeared. The Devonian period is known as the age of fishes. Amphibians and cone-bearing plants also developed during the Devonian period.

© Houghton Mifflin Harcourt Publishing Company

The Carboniferous period, sometimes divided into the Mississippian and Pennsylvanian periods, began 354 million years ago. During this time, amphibians flourished, forests and swamps covered most of the land, and reptiles appeared. The final period in the Paleozoic era was the Permian period. It began around 299 million years ago. The Permian period was characterized by mass extinctions, which marked the end of the Paleozoic era.

The Mesozoic Era

The Mesozoic era is the second oldest era in the Phanerozoic eon. The Mesozoic era began with the Triassic period around 250 million years ago. Both dinosaurs and mammals appeared during the Triassic period.

The Triassic period was followed by the Jurassic period, beginning around 200 million years ago. Dinosaurs dominated the Triassic period. Primitive birds and flying reptiles also appeared during the Jurassic period.

The last period in the Mesozoic era was the Cretaceous period. The Cretaceous period began around 144 million years ago. Flowering plants and modern birds had appeared by this time. The Mesozoic era ended around 65 million years ago with another round of mass extinctions.

The Cenozoic Era

The Cenozoic era is the current era. It is divided into two periods, the Tertiary period and the Quaternary period, which are further divided into epochs and ages.

The Paleocene epoch is the first epoch in the Tertiary period. The Paleocene epoch began around 65 million years ago and marks the beginning of the age of mammals. The first primates appeared during the Paleocene epoch. The Eocene epoch began around 55 million years ago. It was marked by the appearance of horses, flying squirrels, bats, and whales. The Oligocene epoch began around 34 million years ago. It was marked by the appearance of deer, pigs, horses, and camels. The Miocene epoch began 23 million years ago and was marked by the abundance of grazing herds and the appearance of raccoons and wolves. The final epoch in the Tertiary period was the Pliocene epoch. It began around 5 million years ago and was marked by the appearance of large carnivores such as bears and lions.

The Quaternary period has consisted of two epochs: the Pleistocene epoch and the Holocene epoch. The Pleistocene epoch began around 2 million years ago. The Pleistocene epoch was marked by the first appearance of humans. The Holocene epoch is the current epoch. It began around 12,000 years ago. The Holocene epoch marked the end of the last glacial period and the beginning of complex human societies.

© Houghton Mifflin Harcourt Publishing Company

What Is the Geologic Time Scale?

Fill in the blanks.

1. _____ is the study of the formation, history, materials, and processes of the physical Earth.

2. The Cambrian _____ is a time when most modern animal groups appeared.

3. The _____ eon is the youngest eon.

4. The _____ epoch marked the beginning of the age of mammals.

5. All fossils on Earth are part of the _____.

6. The _____ epoch is the current epoch.

7. The Triassic period was part of the _____ era.

8. **Main Idea** What is the geologic time scale?

   _____

   _____

   _____

9. **Vocabulary** Write a paragraph explaining how the geologic time scale is divided using the terms *eon*, *era*, *period*, *epoch*, and *age*.

   _____

   _____

   _____

10. **Reading Skill: Compare** What is the major similarity between the Permian period and the Cretaceous period?

   _____

   _____

© Houghton Mifflin Harcourt Publishing Company

11. Critical Thinking: Infer Why is the geologic time scale divided based on major events in Earth's history instead of set lengths of time?

_____

_____

_____

_____

_____

12. Inquiry Skill: Use Models Draw a diagram to model the geologic time scale.

13. Test Prep Which of the following correctly states the current era, period, and epoch?

   A Cenozoic, Quaternary, Holocene

   B Mesozoic, Triassic, Cretaceous

   C Cenozoic, Tertiary, Pleistocene

   D Cenozoic, Tertiary, Holocene

© Houghton Mifflin Harcourt Publishing Company

How Does Earth Change?

The Geosphere

The solid part of Earth that consists of all rock, as well as the soils and loose rocks on Earth's surface, makes up the geosphere. Forces within the geosphere affect living and nonliving things. When Earth formed about 4.6 billion years ago, its interior was heated by radioactive decay and gravitational contraction. Since that time, the amount of heat generated by radioactive decay has declined. But the decay of radioactive atoms still generates enough heat to keep Earth's interior hot. Earth's interior also retains much of the energy from the planet's formation.

Because Earth's interior is warmer than its surface layers, hot materials move toward the surface in a process called convection. As material is heated, its density decreases, and the hot material rises and releases heat. Cooler, denser material sinks and displaces the hot material. As a result, the heat in Earth's interior is transferred through the layers of Earth and is released at Earth's surface. On a large scale, this process drives the motions in the surface layers of the geosphere that create mountain ranges and ocean basins.

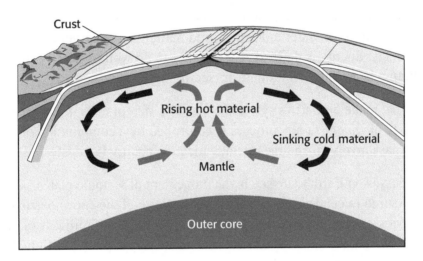

Earth's Layers

Direct observation of Earth's interior has been limited to the upper few kilometers that can be reached by drilling. Scientists must rely on indirect methods to study Earth at greater depths. For example, scientists have made important discoveries about Earth's interior through studies of seismic waves. Seismic waves are vibrations that produce earthquakes. By studying how these waves travel through Earth, scientists have determined that Earth can be divided up into layers based on two characteristics: chemical composition and overall structure. The three compositional layers are the crust, mantle, and core. The five structural layers are the lithosphere, asthenosphere, mesosphere, outer core, and inner core.

The thin, solid, outermost layer of Earth is called the crust. The crust makes up only 1% of Earth's mass. The crust beneath the oceans is called oceanic crust. Oceanic crust is only 5 to 10 km thick. The part of the crust that makes up the continents is called continental crust. Continental crust varies from 15 to 80 km thick. It is thickest beneath high mountain ranges.

53

Earth Science
Core Skills Science, Grade 7

The mantle, the layer under the crust, is denser than the crust. The mantle is nearly 2,900 km thick and makes up almost two-thirds of Earth's mass. The uppermost part of the mantle is cool and brittle. This part of the mantle and the crust above it make up the lithosphere, a rigid layer 15 to 300 km thick. Below the lithosphere is a less rigid layer called the asthenosphere. It is about 200 km thick. Because of enormous heat and pressure, the solid rock of the asthenosphere flows. The ability of a solid to flow is called plasticity. The mesosphere is beneath the asthenosphere. The mesosphere is stronger than the asthenosphere. This means that the rock in the mesosphere does not flow as quickly as rock in the asthenosphere.

Beneath the mantle is the dense, center layer of Earth, called the core, which makes up nearly one-third of Earth's mass. The core is composed mainly of iron and nickel. It is divided into the liquid outer core and the solid inner core.

Earth's Systems

A large and complex system, such as the Earth system, operates as a result of the combination of smaller, interrelated systems. The operation of the Earth system is a result of interaction between the two most basic components of the universe: matter and energy. Matter is anything that has mass and takes up space. Matter can be subatomic particles, such as protons, electrons, and neutrons. Matter can be atoms or molecules, such as oxygen atoms or water molecules, and matter can be larger objects, such as rocks, living organisms, or planets. Energy is defined as the ability to do work. Energy can be transferred in a variety of forms, including heat, light, vibrations, or electromagnetic waves.

The natural processes that make up Earth's systems occur at different rates, ranging from seconds to billions of years. The rate of change of any process is controlled by a combination of the amount of energy that is transferred, the mass involved, and the rate at which the energy is transferred.

One of the slowest processes on Earth's surface is the movement of tectonic plates. The motion of the plates is very slow, measured in centimeters per year; yet because of the enormous mass of the moving continents, tectonic processes can build large mountains over a period of millions of years. Even though the motion of the plates is slow, some tectonic processes occur very rapidly. Earthquakes are caused by sudden movements that can occur in seconds or less.

Explosive volcanic eruptions can rapidly eject large amounts of rock and gases. This occurs when a large amount of potential energy builds over time and is suddenly changed into kinetic energy. The potential energy builds as pressure on the crust increases because of the slow movement of tectonic plates.

Weathering is the wearing down of the materials of Earth's crust. Erosion is the removal of weathered sediments. Erosion can occur over millions of years. For example, the Grand Canyon was formed by water wearing away rock over a long period. Other erosion processes can occur very rapidly. Flash floods and large landslides can happen in seconds or minutes, often without warning. Like earthquakes and volcanic eruptions, these processes occur as potential energy builds and is suddenly released, causing water or land to move.

Other Earth systems change constantly as well, and the rate of change depends on the rate of energy transfer. For example, climate change is generally a slow process but occurs faster as greenhouse gases increase the amount of solar energy absorbed by the atmosphere. Ecosystems are generally fairly stable, changing slowly, but when one part of the system is changed suddenly, the flow of energy and matter in the system can be altered and the entire system may undergo rapid change.

© Houghton Mifflin Harcourt Publishing Company

How Does Earth Change?

Write the answers to the questions on the lines below.

1. What process drives the motions in the surface layers of the geosphere that form mountain ranges and ocean basins?

   _____

2. What is the geosphere?

   _____

   _____

3. How old is Earth? _____

4. When construction workers dig into the ground, which structural layer of Earth's geosphere are they digging in?

   _____

5. Which structural layer of Earth's interior have scientists concluded is liquid?

   _____

6. Correctly list Earth's structural layers from deepest to shallowest.

   _____

   _____

7. What is matter? What is energy?

   _____

   _____

8. What is erosion?

   _____

9. **Main Idea** How can the cycling of matter and energy in the Earth system lead to movement in Earth's crust?

   _____

   _____

© Houghton Mifflin Harcourt Publishing Company

10. Vocabulary Describe the chemical and structural layers of Earth using the terms *lithosphere*, *asthenosphere, mesosphere, inner core, outer core, crust, mantle,* and *core.*

_____

_____

_____

_____

11. Reading Skill: Main Idea and Details How are scientists able to determine the composition and size of Earth's layers?

_____

_____

12. Critical Thinking: Synthesize Describe changes to Earth's crust through weathering and tectonic processes that can happen very slowly and very quickly.

_____

_____

_____

_____

13. Inquiry Skill: Use Models Draw a diagram to model the layers of Earth. Be sure to include both the structural and compositional layers. If possible, draw the layers to scale. Identify in which layer(s) convection occurs.

14. Test Prep Which of the following statements regarding Earth's interior is true?

 A Earth's interior retains little of the heat produced during Earth's formation.

 B Radioactive decay occurs at a higher rate now than it did during Earth's formation.

 C Radioactive decay has decreased since Earth's formation but still heats Earth's interior.

 D Earth's interior was once heated by radioactive decay but is now heated by gravitational contraction.

© Houghton Mifflin Harcourt Publishing Company

What Is the Rock Cycle?

Classes of Rocks

Geologists place all rocks into three major classes. These classes are based on how the rocks form. The three major classes of rocks are sedimentary, igneous, and metamorphic. Sedimentary rocks form when rocks break into smaller pieces, and those pieces become cemented together. Igneous rocks form when hot, liquid rock—called magma—cools and becomes solid. Metamorphic rocks form when rock is changed because of chemical processes or changes in temperature and pressure. Each class of rock can be further classified into rock types based on composition and texture.

Sedimentary Rock

Sedimentary rocks are divided into three types: clastic, chemical, and organic. Clastic sedimentary rocks are made of fragments of rock or minerals. Before they are cemented together, these fragments of rock or minerals are called sediment. Clastic sedimentary rocks form when sediments are buried, put under pressure, and cemented by minerals such as calcite and quartz. Chemical sedimentary rocks form when minerals crystallize from a solution, such as ocean water. The minerals are buried, put under pressure, and cemented together. Organic sedimentary rocks form when the shells and skeletons of dead marine animals are buried and cemented by calcite or quartz. Limestone is a sedimentary rock made of calcite. Conglomerate is a sedimentary rock made of pieces of quartz and feldspar cemented together.

Igneous Rock

Igneous rocks are divided into groups based on the texture of the rock or the size of the crystals in the rock. Magma that slowly cools deep inside Earth forms coarse-grained rocks made of large crystals. Lava that erupts at Earth's surface and quickly cools forms fine-grained rocks made of very small crystals. Igneous rock can also be classified by its chemical composition. The chemical composition of an igneous rock is determined by the type of rock that initially melts to form magma. Magma from melted crustal material tends to form light-colored igneous rocks, such as granite. Magma from Earth's mantle forms dark-colored igneous rocks, such as basalt. Basalt is an igneous rock made of feldspar, pyroxene, and olivine. Granite is an igneous rock made of quartz and feldspar.

Metamorphic Rock

Metamorphic rock is rock that forms from other rocks as a result of intense heat, pressure, or chemical processes. Most metamorphic changes happen deep within Earth's crust at depths greater than 2 km. At these depths, pressure can be many times greater than it is at Earth's surface. Temperature is also much higher at these depths than it is at Earth's surface. There are two types of metamorphic rocks. The minerals of foliated metamorphic rock, such as gneiss, are arranged in planes or bands. The minerals of nonfoliated metamorphic rock, such as marble, are not arranged in planes or bands.

© Houghton Mifflin Harcourt Publishing Company

The Rock Cycle

The rock cycle describes how rocks constantly change from one form to another. For example, a sedimentary rock can be weathered and eroded into sediments. The sediments can be exposed to high temperature and heat, forming a metamorphic rock. Alternatively, they can be buried and melted, then cool and harden to form an igneous rock, or they can be compressed and cemented together to form another sedimentary rock. In this way, rocks are recycled and matter is conserved.

- Sedimentary rock can change into a new sedimentary rock when sediments are weathered and eroded and then compacted and cemented together.

- Sedimentary rock can change into metamorphic rock under intense temperatures and pressure.

- Sedimentary rock can change into igneous rock through melting and cooling.

- Metamorphic rock can change into sedimentary rock when sediments are weathered and eroded and then compacted and cemented together.

- Metamorphic rock can change into new metamorphic rock under intense temperatures and pressure.

- Metamorphic rock can change into igneous rock through melting and cooling.

- Igneous rock can change into sedimentary rock when sediments are weathered and eroded and then compacted and cemented together.

- Igneous rock can change into metamorphic rock under intense temperatures and pressure.

- Igneous rock can change into new igneous rock through melting and cooling.

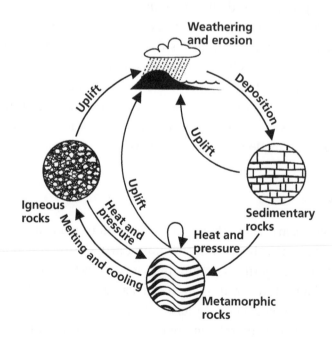

© Houghton Mifflin Harcourt Publishing Company

What Is the Rock Cycle?

Write the answers to the questions on the lines below.

1. Which sedimentary rock is formed by calcite?

_____

2. Describe how granite forms.

_____

3. What is required to transform a sedimentary rock into a metamorphic rock?

_____

_____

4. Describe how limestone forms.

_____

_____

5. What characteristic do geologists use to classify rocks into the three major classes?

_____

6. Describe how marble forms.

_____

7. What is the rock cycle?

_____

_____

8. Main Idea What are the three types of rock involved in the rock cycle?

_____

_____

_____

© Houghton Mifflin Harcourt Publishing Company

9. Vocabulary Write a paragraph describing how a rock could move through the rock cycle using the terms *metamorphic*, *igneous*, and *sedimentary*.

_____

_____

_____

_____

10. Reading Skill: Main Idea and Details What type of rock forms when heat and pressure change the structure, textures, or composition of sedimentary rock?

_____

_____

11. Critical Thinking: Synthesize Use the rock cycle to explain conservation of matter.

_____

_____

_____

12. Inquiry Skill: Infer How can basalt become a sedimentary rock?

_____

_____

_____

13. Test Prep According to the rock cycle, which of the following steps is necessary for sedimentary rock to form?

A heat and pressure

B melting and cooling

C compaction and cementation

D volcanic activity

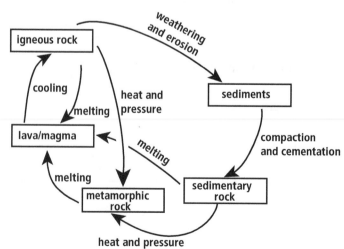

© Houghton Mifflin Harcourt Publishing Company

How Does Water Cycle on Earth?

Water on Earth

Earth stands out from the other planets in our solar system primarily for one reason—71% of Earth's surface is covered with water. Most of Earth's water is found in the global ocean. The ocean is a unique body of water that plays many parts in regulating Earth's environment. The largest ocean is the Pacific Ocean.

There is a limited amount of fresh water on Earth. Only 3% of Earth's water is drinkable. And of the 3% of Earth's water that is drinkable, 77% is frozen in the polar ice caps. Much of Earth's liquid water is contained in watersheds. A river system is made up of a network of streams and rivers. A watershed is a region that collects runoff water that then becomes part of a river or a lake. Erosion by both rivers and oceans can produce dramatic changes on Earth's surface and give rise to a variety of spectacular landforms.

Although you can see some of Earth's water in streams and lakes, you cannot see the large amount of water that percolates underground. The water located within the rocks below Earth's surface is called groundwater. A permeable rock layer that stores groundwater and allows the flow of groundwater is called an aquifer. An aquifer can be described by its ability to hold water and its ability to allow water to pass freely through it. The amount of available water in an aquifer depends on multiple factors, including how much water is used, how quickly the water is replenished, what changes take place on the ground surface, and temperature.

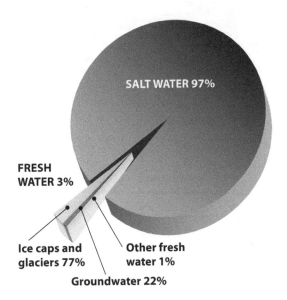

SALT WATER 97%

FRESH WATER 3%

Ice caps and glaciers 77%

Other fresh water 1%

Groundwater 22%

The Hydrosphere

The hydrosphere makes up all of the water on or near Earth's surface. Much of this water is in the oceans. Water is also found in the atmosphere, on land, and in the soil. The hydrosphere interacts with both the atmosphere and geosphere, as well as with living things. The continuous movement of water between oceans, atmosphere, land, and living things is known as the water cycle.

© Houghton Mifflin Harcourt Publishing Company

The Water Cycle

Water continuously cycles between Earth's surface and atmosphere in a process called the water cycle. The water cycle involves the processes of evaporation, transpiration, condensation, and precipitation.

During evaporation, the sun's energy causes liquid water to change into a gas called water vapor. When water evaporates from the leaves of plants, the process is called transpiration.

As the water vapor rises into the atmosphere, it cools and changes back to liquid droplets. This process is called condensation. Millions of tiny droplets join together to form a cloud. Some water droplets become too heavy to remain aloft, and they fall to Earth's surface as precipitation. The precipitation that falls on land and flows into bodies of water is called runoff. Some precipitation seeps into the ground and is stored in spaces between or within rocks. This water, called groundwater, slowly flows back into rivers and eventually oceans.

Water frozen in glaciers takes a long time to rejoin the water cycle. It does not evaporate or run off until a glacier melts.

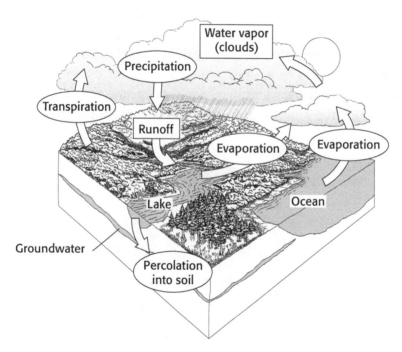

Human Impact on the Water Cycle

Human activities can affect the quality of water as it flows through the water cycle. For example, acid rain forms when pollutants from burning fossil fuels lower the pH of precipitation to the point that it can harm plants, forests, and aquatic ecosystems. Humans can also impact the water cycle by using up too much groundwater or surface water. This can change the patterns of evaporation, condensation, and precipitation, as well as affect the access of other organisms to fresh water.

© Houghton Mifflin Harcourt Publishing Company

How Does Water Cycle on Earth?

Match each definition to its term.

Definitions   **Terms**

_____ 1. all of the water on or near Earth's surface   **a.** aquifer

_____ 2. water droplets that fall to Earth's surface   **b.** hydrosphere

_____ 3. water evaporation from the leaves of plants   **c.** condensation

_____ 4. added energy causes liquid water to change to gaseous water vapor **d.** water cycle

_____ 5. water vapor cools and changes to liquid droplets   **e.** transpiration

_____ 6. permeable rock layer that stores groundwater   **f.** evaporation

_____ 7. continuous movement of water between atmosphere, oceans, land,   **g.** precipitation
          and living things

8. **Main Idea** Oceans are a key part of Earth's water cycle. Which process in the water cycle takes place largely over the oceans? Explain.

_____

_____

_____

_____

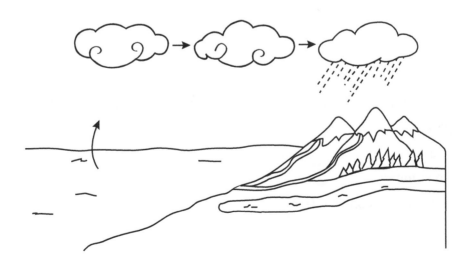

© Houghton Mifflin Harcourt Publishing Company

Earth Science
Core Skills Science, Grade 7

9. **Vocabulary** Write a paragraph describing the water cycle using the terms *transpiration*, *evaporation*, *condensation*, and *precipitation*.

_____

_____

_____

_____

10. **Reading Skill: Main Idea and Details** By what process do clouds form in the atmosphere?

_____

_____

11. **Critical Thinking: Analyze** What role does the sun play in the water cycle?

_____

_____

_____

12. **Inquiry Skill: Use Models** Create a diagram that models the path a drop of water in a puddle could take through the water cycle.

13. **Test Prep** At what point during the water cycle does water vapor gain energy?

   A during evaporation

   B during condensation

   C during precipitation

   D during evaporation and condensation

© Houghton Mifflin Harcourt Publishing Company

What Is Weather?

Weather

When you wake up in the morning, do you ever wonder about the conditions outside? For example, is it hot or cold outside? Wet or dry? Cloudy and stormy or clear and calm? All of these conditions are aspects of the local weather. Weather is the state of the atmosphere at a specific place and time. Weather events are caused by differences in air pressure, which are influenced by several factors, such as energy from the sun, latitude, and elevation. Oceans play a large role in Earth's weather because they absorb, store, and redistribute energy from the sun. This energy drives weather systems across Earth's surface.

Weather Fronts

The area in which two types of air masses meet is called a front. There are four kinds of fronts—cold fronts, warm fronts, occluded fronts, and stationary fronts. Fronts are associated with weather in the middle latitudes.

A cold front forms where cold air moves under warm air, which is less dense, and pushes the warm air up. Cold fronts can move quickly and bring thunderstorms, heavy rain, or snow. Cooler weather usually follows a cold front because the air mass behind the cold front is cooler and drier than the air mass that it is replacing.

A warm front forms where warm air moves over cold, denser air. In a warm front, the warm air gradually replaces the cold air. Warm fronts generally bring drizzly rain and are followed by clear and warm weather.

An occluded front forms when a warm air mass is caught between two colder air masses. The coldest air mass moves under and pushes up the warm air mass. The coldest air mass then moves forward until it meets a cold air mass that is warmer and less dense. The colder of these two air masses moves under and pushes up the warmer air mass. Sometimes, though, the two colder air masses mix. An occluded front has cool temperatures and large amounts of rain and snow.

A stationary front forms when a cold air mass meets a warm air mass. In this case, however, neither air mass has enough force to move the other, so the two air masses remain separated. This may happen because there is not enough wind to keep the air masses pushing against each other. A stationary front often brings many days of cloudy, wet weather.

© Houghton Mifflin Harcourt Publishing Company

Hurricanes

A large, rotating tropical weather system that has wind speeds of at least 120 km/h is called a hurricane. Hurricanes are the most powerful storms on Earth. Hurricanes have different names in different parts of the world. In the western Pacific Ocean, hurricanes are called typhoons. Hurricanes that form over the Indian Ocean are called cyclones. Hurricanes vary in size from 160 to 1,500 km in diameter and can travel for thousands of kilometers.

A hurricane begins as a group of thunderstorms moving over warm, tropical ocean waters. Winds traveling in two different directions meet and cause the storm to spin. Because of the Coriolis effect, the storm turns counterclockwise in the Northern Hemisphere and clockwise in the Southern Hemisphere.

A hurricane gets its energy from the condensation of water vapor. Once formed, the hurricane is fueled through contact with the warm ocean water. Moisture is added to the warm air by evaporation from the ocean. As the warm, moist air rises, the water vapor condenses and releases large amounts of energy. The hurricane continues to grow as long as it is over its source of warm, moist air. When the hurricane moves into colder waters or over land, it begins to die because it has lost its source of energy.

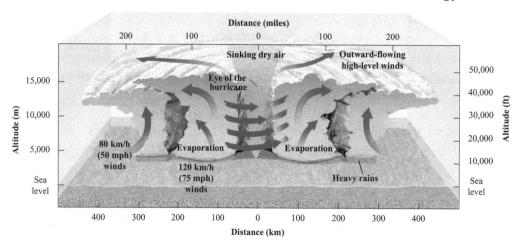

Forecasting Weather

Meteorology is the study of the atmosphere, which includes weather phenomena. To forecast the weather, meteorologists need to measure various atmospheric conditions, such as air pressure, humidity, precipitation, temperature, wind speed, and wind direction. Meteorologists use simple tools such as barometers and thermometers as well as more sophisticated tools such as weather satellites and Doppler radar. Computers use the collected data to model possible weather patterns. Computer models can show possible weather conditions for several days. However, meteorologists must carefully interpret these models because computer predictions are based on generalized descriptions.

Meteorologists interpret data to make five types of forecasts. Nowcasts mainly use radar and enable forecasters to focus on timing precipitation and tracking severe weather. Daily forecasts predict weather conditions for a 48-hour period. Extended forecasts look ahead 3 to 7 days. Medium-range forecasts look ahead 8 to 14 days. Long-range forecasts cover monthly and seasonal periods.

Weather forecasts are not always accurate. The conditions that govern weather are so complex that weather can only be predicted, often with varying degrees of accuracy.

© Houghton Mifflin Harcourt Publishing Company

Earth Science
Core Skills Science, Grade 7

What Is Weather?

Write the answers to the questions on the lines below.

1. Which type of forecast do you think would be most accurate? Why?

   _____

2. Where do hurricanes build strength?

   _____

   _____

3. What kind of weather does a cold front usually bring?

   _____

   _____

4. What is the minimum wind speed in km/h for a system to be classified as a hurricane?

   _____

5. What is the source of energy that fuels large storms such as hurricanes?

   _____

   _____

6. What is meteorology?

   _____

7. What is a typhoon?

   _____

8. Why do hurricanes lose strength as they move onto land from the ocean?

   _____

   _____

© Houghton Mifflin Harcourt Publishing Company

9. Main Idea What is weather?

_____

_____

10. Vocabulary Write a paragraph describing the four main types of fronts using the terms *cold front*, *warm front*, *occluded front*, and *stationary front*.

thunder storms

low air pressure inside funnel

warm air

funnel cloud

_____

_____

_____

_____

11. Reading Skill: Compare and Contrast Compare and contrast the five types of weather forecasts.

_____

_____

12. Critical Thinking: Evaluate Explain the role oceans play in Earth's weather.

_____

_____

_____

13. Inquiry Skill: Use Models Create a graphic organizer, such as a flowchart or concept map, that shows how a weather forecast is developed.

14. Test Prep What kind of front forms when a cold air mass displaces a warm air mass?

    A a cold front

    B a warm front

    C an occluded front

    D a stationary front

© Houghton Mifflin Harcourt Publishing Company

What Are Minerals?

Minerals

Mineralogy is the study of minerals. A mineral is a natural, usually inorganic solid that has a characteristic chemical composition, an orderly internal structure, and a characteristic set of physical properties. The physical properties of minerals include color, density, streak, luster, cleavage, fracture, and hardness. Streak describes the color of a mineral in powder form. Luster describes how a mineral reflects light. Cleavage and fracture describe how a mineral breaks. Hardness describes how hard a mineral is.

Identifying Minerals

If you closed your eyes and tasted different foods, you could probably determine what the foods are by noting properties such as saltiness or sweetness. You can also determine the identity of a mineral by noting different properties. The same mineral can come in a variety of colors. For example, in its purest state, quartz is clear. Samples of quartz that contain various types and amounts of impurities, however, can be a variety of colors. Besides impurities, other factors can change the appearance of minerals. The mineral pyrite, often called fool's gold, normally has a golden color. But if pyrite is exposed to air and water for a long period, it can turn brown or black. Because of factors such as impurities, color usually is not the best way to identify a mineral.

The way a surface reflects light is called luster. When you say an object is shiny or dull, you are describing its luster. Minerals have metallic, submetallic, or nonmetallic luster. If a mineral is shiny, it has a metallic luster. If the mineral is dull, its luster is either submetallic or nonmetallic.

The color of a mineral in powdered form is called the mineral's streak. A mineral's streak can be found by rubbing the mineral against a piece of unglazed porcelain called a streak plate. The mark left on the streak plate is
the streak. The streak is a thin layer of powdered mineral. The color of a mineral's streak is not always the same as the color of the mineral sample. Unlike the surface of a mineral sample, the streak is not affected by air or water. For this reason, using streak is more reliable than using color in identifying a mineral.

© Houghton Mifflin Harcourt Publishing Company

A mineral's resistance to being scratched is called hardness. To determine the hardness of minerals, scientists use Mohs hardness scale. The greater a mineral's resistance to being scratched is, the higher the mineral's rating is. To identify a mineral by using Mohs hardness scale, try to scratch the surface of a mineral with the edge of one of the reference minerals. If the reference mineral scratches your mineral, the reference mineral is harder than your mineral.

Density is the measure of how much matter is in a given amount of space. In other words, density is a ratio of an object's mass to its volume. Because water has a density of $1 g/cm^3$, it is used as a reference point for other substances. The ratio of an object's density to the density of water is called the object's specific gravity.

Mohs Hardness Scale	
Minerals	**Hardness**
Talc	1
Gypsum	2
Calcite	3
Fluorite	4
Apatite	5
Feldspar	6
Quartz	7
Topaz	8
Corundum	9
Diamond	10

Minerals and Rocks

Minerals are not the same as rocks. The material that makes up the solid parts of Earth is known as rock. Rocks can be a collection of one or more minerals, or rock can be made of solid organic matter, such as coal. In some cases, rock is made of mineral matter that is not crystalline, such as glass. As you learned in "What Is the Rock Cycle?", rocks are classified according to how they formed.

Human Use of Minerals

Minerals are a nonrenewable natural resource that come from the environment. Both minerals and rocks are mined for human use. Mineral resources can be either metals, such as gold, silver, and aluminum, or nonmetals, such as sulfur and quartz. Some metals are prized for their beauty and rarity. Certain rare nonmetallic minerals called gemstones display extraordinary brilliance and color when they are specifically cut for jewelry. Other nonmetallic minerals, such as calcite and gypsum, are used as building materials. Table salt is derived from the nonmetallic mineral halite. The distribution of minerals across Earth is dependent upon Earth processes, such as the rock cycle and volcanism, as well as the chemical composition of Earth. This means that minerals, like other resources, are distributed unevenly around the globe. Mineral deposits on land fall within the national borders of particular countries. Only these countries can mine the mineral deposits. For this reason, the wealth obtained from mining precious metals and gemstones is also distributed unevenly around the globe.

© Houghton Mifflin Harcourt Publishing Company

What Are Minerals?

Write the answers to the questions on the lines below.

1. What information can a mineralogist learn from testing the mass and volume of a mineral?

   _____

2. What is the name for the tendency of a mineral to break, creating a new smooth edge?

   _____

3. How would you determine the hardness of a mineral?

   _____

   _____

   _____

4. What is luster?

   _____

5. How would you determine the streak of a mineral?

   _____

   _____

6. Why is color not a good characteristic for identifying minerals?

   _____

   _____

7. What is specific gravity?

   _____

   _____

8. **Main Idea** Compare a rock and a mineral.

   _____

   _____

© Houghton Mifflin Harcourt Publishing Company

9. **Vocabulary** Write a paragraph describing the physical properties of minerals using the terms *luster*, *streak*, *hardness*, *cleavage*, and *density*.

_____

_____

_____

_____

10. **Reading Skill: Main Idea and Details** How do humans use minerals?

_____

_____

_____

_____

11. **Critical Thinking: Analyze** A scientist tests the hardness of a mineral and finds that it can scratch feldspar, but not corundum. Which other minerals share this property? Use the Mohs hardness scale to find your answer.

_____

_____

_____

_____

12. **Inquiry Skill: Infer** Explain how the uneven distribution of minerals around the world can impact local economies.

_____

_____

_____

_____

13. **Test Prep** According to the Mohs hardness scale for minerals, which of the following minerals is the hardest?

A fluorite

B quartz

C calcite

D feldspar

© Houghton Mifflin Harcourt Publishing Company

What Are Natural Hazards?

Natural Hazards

Natural processes that can change ecosystems include natural disasters, such as earthquakes and volcanic eruptions, and extreme weather such as floods, droughts, hurricanes, and tornadoes. All of these events can be considered natural hazards that can cause the loss of ecosystems, property, and human life.

Volcanic Eruptions and Earthquakes

A volcano is a mountain with a vent that leads to molten rock within Earth. Volcanic eruptions can cause the loss of human life and can devastate wildlife habitats. During an eruption, pyroclastic flows can race down the slope of a volcano and burn everything in their path. The hot volcanic materials can melt the snowcap on a mountain, which can cause devastating floods. Volcanic ash can mix with water to produce lahars, fast-moving mudflows that bury everything in their way. The weight of falling ash can collapse structures, bury crops, and damage engines.

An earthquake is a sudden movement of Earth's crust. Earthquakes occur along the boundaries of tectonic plates. Energy is released during an earthquake and seismic waves are created. The energy in the seismic waves can cause damage to ecosystems and human property. Movements in Earth's crust are monitored with seismometers, and earthquakes can be measured using the Richter scale.

If the center of an earthquake occurs offshore, or under the ocean, a large tidal wave, or tsunami, may form. Tsunamis are long water waves that can be very destructive. Depending on the location of the undersea earthquake, tsunamis can make landfall minutes, or even hours, after a large earthquake.

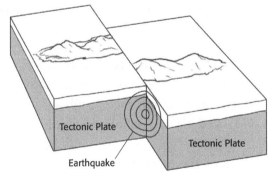

Tectonic Plate

Tectonic Plate

Earthquake

Mass Movement

Gravity causes rock fragments to move downhill. This movement of fragments down a slope is called mass movement. The most dramatic and destructive mass movements occur rapidly. The fall of rock from a steep cliff is called a rockfall. A rockfall is the fastest kind of mass movement. Rocks in rockfalls often range in size from tiny fragments to giant boulders. When masses of loose rock combined with soil suddenly fall down a slope, the event is called a landslide. Large landslides in which loosened blocks of bedrock fall generally occur on very steep slopes. Heavy rainfall, spring thaws, volcanic eruptions, and earthquakes can trigger landslides.

The rapid movement of a large amount of mud creates a mudflow. Mudflows occur in dry, mountainous regions during sudden heavy rainfall or as a result of volcanic eruptions. Mud churns and tumbles as it moves down slopes and through valleys, and it frequently spreads out in a large fan shape at the base of a slope. Sometimes, a large block of soil and rock becomes unstable and moves downhill in one piece. The block of soil then slides along the curved slope of the surface. This type of movement is called a slump. Slumping occurs along very steep slopes. Saturation by water and loss of friction with underlying rock causes slumping.

© Houghton Mifflin Harcourt Publishing Company

Severe Weather

There are many types of severe weather on Earth that can result in natural hazards. Severe thunderstorms can cause damaging winds and hail, lightning, flash floods, and even tornadoes. Floods are natural events that happen in recurring patterns. These natural events can cause a great deal of damage. Wildlife habitats can be buried or washed away. Human property may be damaged. The flooding of the Mississippi River in 1993 caused damage in nine states. Farms were destroyed, and whole towns were evacuated.

A tornado is a funnel of rotating air that is in contact with the ground and the base of a storm cloud. Tornadoes can range in size, shape, and duration. They are characterized by violent winds that can reach up to 250 miles per hour. Tornadoes can cause massive damage to ecosystems and human property. Tornadoes are also responsible for the loss of human life every year.

Forecasting Natural Hazards

Scientists study all types of natural hazards in an effort to forecast their occurrence, predict their effects, and prevent some of the losses that occur due to natural hazards. Some natural hazards are easier to forecast than others.

Scientists monitor activity within Earth's crust with seismometers. Scientists cannot accurately forecast the occurrence of one particular earthquake or a volcanic eruption. However, as scientists monitor a particular area over a long period of time, they can begin to form baselines of seismic activity. This helps scientists pinpoint unusual activity, and can possibly lead to advanced warning of a volcanic eruption or large earthquake.

Scientists monitor severe weather using satellites, Doppler radar, and on the ground observations. Some storms, such as hurricanes, form relatively slowly. Scientists track these storms over days and even weeks. Affected populations receive advance notice of these storms making landfall, so destruction of property and loss of life can be minimized. However, there are some natural hazards, such as tornadoes, that form very quickly. Scientists may only be able to give a few minutes advance notice that a tornado has been sighted on the ground. In the United States, the National Weather Service has a system of watches and warnings that can be issued to specific areas based on the likelihood of severe weather occurring. This warning system has saved many lives by giving people more time to seek shelter from severe weather. Also, scientists now understand that storms such as hurricanes and tornadoes occur more frequently in specific regions. This understanding allows scientists to make recommendations for building codes and storm shelter availability in communities that may be affected the most by severe weather.

Although some mass movements are unpredictable and, therefore, unpreventable, others can be avoided. Geologists locate areas where mass movements have occurred, try to identify landforms and soils prone to mass movement, and look for signs of potential slump, creep, or other movement. They use this information to create landslide potential maps that show regions susceptible to mass movement. If signs of movement are detected or land is prone to movement, common sense suggests not building there. If the area is already developed, steps can be taken to restabilize the slope. For example, barren slopes can be replanted, or terraces and retaining walls can be constructed.

© Houghton Mifflin Harcourt Publishing Company

What Are Natural Hazards?

Match each definition to its term.

Definitions   **Terms**

_____ **1.** sudden movement of Earth's crust   **a.** rockfall

_____ **2.** rotating funnel of air that is in contact with the ground and   **b.** mass movement
a storm cloud
                                                                  c. slumping
_____ **3.** fall of rock from a steep cliff
                                                                  d. tsunami
_____ **4.** movement of fragments down a slope
                                                                  e. earthquake
_____ **5.** rapid movement of a large amount of mud
                                                                  f. landslide
_____ **6.** large tidal wave
                                                                  g. tornado
_____ **7.** masses of loose rock and soil fall down a slope
                                                                  h. mudflow
_____ **8.** large block of soil and rock moves downhill in one piece

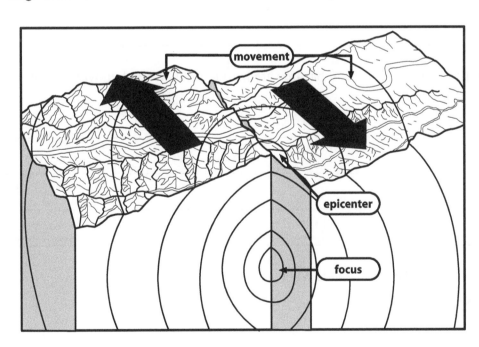

9. Main Idea Why do scientists study natural hazards?

_____

_____

_____

© Houghton Mifflin Harcourt Publishing Company

10. **Vocabulary** Write a paragraph describing natural hazards using the terms *earthquake*, *volcano*, *tornado*, and *mass movement*.

_____

_____

_____

_____

11. **Reading Skill: Main Idea and Details** What can be done to prevent mass movements?

_____

_____

_____

12. **Critical Thinking: Identify Cause and Effect** Describe the causes and effects of a mudflow.

_____

_____

_____

13. **Inquiry Skill: Infer** Many natural hazards are hard to predict. Explain why this makes natural hazards so dangerous.

_____

_____

_____

_____

14. **Test Prep** Which of the following is **NOT** a natural hazard?

    A earthquake

    B volcano

    C high tide

    D tornado

© Houghton Mifflin Harcourt Publishing Company

How Do Humans Impact Earth?

Earth consists of rock, air, water, and living things that all interact. Scientists divide this system into four parts: the geosphere (rock), the atmosphere (air), the hydrosphere (water), and the biosphere (living things). Humans cause many changes to the Earth system, from polluting the atmosphere and the hydrosphere to destroying parts of the biosphere and geosphere. There are many problems that can affect the survival of individuals and entire species in an ecosystem. The following factors can negatively affect the environment.

Pollution

Pollution is an unwanted change in the environment caused by substances such as wastes or by forms of energy such as radiation. Anything that causes pollution is called a pollutant. Many pollutants are human-made, such as garbage or chemical wastes in water, soil, or the atmosphere.

Air pollutants include carbon monoxide, nitrogen oxide, sulfur dioxide, and volatile organic compounds. Carbon monoxide (CO) is a poisonous, odorless, colorless gas that is released by the incomplete burning of fossil fuels in vehicles and industrial processes. Carbon monoxide interferes with the blood's ability to carry oxygen, causing drowsiness and death. Nitrogen oxide (NO_x) is a gas produced by burning fuels in vehicles, power plants, and industrial boilers when combustion is hotter than 538°C. Nitrogen oxide can contribute to respiratory infections, cancer, smog in cities, and acid rain. Sulfur dioxide (SO_2) is a gas produced by reactions between sulfur and oxygen in the burning of fossil fuels. Sulfur dioxide contributes to acid rain and forms pollutants that harm plants and irritate the respiratory system. Volatile organic compounds (VOCs) are organic chemicals that vaporize to form toxic fumes. VOCs are produced by burning fuels in vehicles. VOCs contribute to smog and can cause serious health problems, such as cancer.

Water pollutants include pathogens and organic matter. Pathogens are disease-causing organisms, such as bacteria, viruses, protozoa, and worms. The primary source of pathogenic pollutants is animal feces from livestock and poultry farms and sewage from wastewater treatment plants. Pathogens cause disease and sometimes death in humans and animals. Organic matter includes animal and plant matter remains, feces, and food waste. The primary source of organic matter pollutants includes mostly nonpoint sources, but can be from farms and food-processing plants. Organic matter is processed through decomposition, which uses oxygen. Systems with increased rates of decomposition may have decreased oxygen availability, which may limit the types of organisms that can survive there.

Resource Depletion

Natural resources in the environment are used to fulfill some need. A renewable resource can be replaced at the same rate it is used. Solar and wind energy are renewable resources, as are some kinds of trees. A nonrenewable resource cannot be replaced or can be replaced only over thousands or millions of years. Most minerals and fossil fuels, such as oil and coal, are nonrenewable resources. When these resources become scarce, humans will have to find other resources to replace them. Fossil fuels are a nonrenewable resource, and the way humans drill and mine for them causes extensive damage to ecosystems. The burning of fossil fuels also causes pollution, such as acid rain.

© Houghton Mifflin Harcourt Publishing Company

Exotic Species

An organism that makes a home for itself in a new place outside its native home is called an exotic species. Exotic species often thrive in new places where they have fewer predators. Some nonnative species are introduced to an ecosystem on purpose. For example, people often cultivate exotic plants for decoration or as crops. Other nonnative species may be introduced to a region as household pets. These pets may later escape or be released into the wild. Still other exotic species might be introduced on purpose in an attempt to control native populations.

Exotic species that thrive in their new homes are often called invasive species. They may not have natural predators in their new environments. They may out-compete native species for limited resources. They may even prey upon native organisms that did not have many native predators before the invasion. When these invaders thrive, they can often cause devastating problems for native species. For example, Burmese pythons brought to Florida as pets have invaded the Florida Everglades—a wetland region that is home to many threatened plant and animal species. The exotic pythons have few natural predators and are reproducing rapidly in their new home. Their presence is a problem in part because they have been known to prey upon native species, such as the endangered Key Largo wood rats.

Habitat Destruction and Fragmentation

When land is cleared so it can be used for construction, crops, mines, or lumber, the topsoil may erode. Chemicals may pollute nearby streams and rivers. The organisms that were living in these areas may be left without food and shelter and may die. An organism's habitat is where it lives. Every habitat has its own number and variety of organisms, or biodiversity. If a habitat is damaged, biodiversity is lost. Habitat fragmentation occurs when human activity makes part of an ecosystem inaccessible.

The world's tropical rainforests are being burned and cut at an alarming rate. However, habitat destruction also happens daily on a smaller scale almost everywhere on Earth. Land is cleared for urban development and agriculture, or large roads are built through habitats. Roads create an impassable barrier for many species, and so habitats are fragmented into smaller pieces.

Human Population Growth

Advances in medicine, such as immunizations, and advances in farming have made human population growth possible. Some people argue that there may eventually be too many people on Earth. Overpopulation occurs when the number of individuals becomes so large that the resources needed for survival are not available to everyone. As the world population increases, the negative human impacts on Earth's systems will also increase. One solution is to engineer technological advances that will help minimize human impact on Earth.

© Houghton Mifflin Harcourt Publishing Company

How Do Humans Impact Earth?

Write the answers to the questions on the lines below.

1. What term describes a species that is not native to a region?

   _____

2. What is a nonrenewable resource?

   _____

   _____

3. What is pollution? _____

   _____

4. What is the difference between an exotic species and an invasive species?

   _____

   _____

5. What are some sources of air pollution?

   _____

   _____

6. How have Burmese pythons affected their new habitat in Florida?

   _____

   _____

7. What is habitat fragmentation?

   _____

   _____

8. **Main Idea** Explain how the growth of the human population can increase human impact on Earth.

   _____

   _____

   _____

© Houghton Mifflin Harcourt Publishing Company

Earth Science
Core Skills Science, Grade 7

9. **Vocabulary** Write a paragraph describing the importance of Earth's natural resources using the terms *renewable* and *nonrenewable*.

_____

_____

_____

_____

10. **Reading Skill: Main Idea and Details** What is one result of humans burning large amounts of fossil fuels?

_____

_____

11. **Critical Thinking: Infer** Noxious weeds are plants that invade ecosystems and grow very quickly and aggressively. How would noxious weeds affect the biodiversity of an ecosystem?

_____

_____

_____

12. **Inquiry Skill: Predict** What will happen to the Earth system if we do not find better ways to minimize human impact?

_____

_____

_____

_____

13. **Test Prep** Imagine that a nonnative bird species appears in an ecosystem. Which of the following will **NOT** be a likely change in the ecosystem?

   A Native bird species will immediately migrate to another area.

   B Bird predator species will temporarily have more available prey.

   C Each food chain in the ecosystem will adjust over time to include the new species of bird.

   D Birds that share the same niche as the new species will have more competition for resources.

© Houghton Mifflin Harcourt Publishing Company

What Is Climate Change?

Climate

Climate is the average weather conditions of an area over a given period of time. Climate is not the same as weather. Weather is short-term atmospheric events that happen on a relatively local scale. Climate is long-term weather patterns that occur on a larger scale, such as a regional or global climate.

Earth's climate is primarily fueled by energy from the sun. Without the warmth from sunlight, life on Earth would not be possible. Energy from the sun is absorbed by the atmosphere, by the oceans, and even by the land on Earth. This energy is distributed unevenly around the globe through convection currents in the atmosphere and in the oceans.

There are natural factors that cause changes to Earth's climate, such as the tilt of Earth's axis or a fluctuation of solar activity. However, it is thought that humans are the largest cause of the climate change Earth is currently experiencing.

Climate Change

Climate change refers to long-term, significant changes to temperatures and weather patterns on a global scale. The National Oceanic and Atmospheric Administration (NOAA) has identified ten indicators of climate. These indicators are: 1) air temperature over land, 2) air temperature over oceans, 3) air temperature of the lower atmosphere, 4) temperature of ocean surface water, 5) ocean heat content, 6) amount of arctic sea ice, 7) amount of glaciation, 8) amount of snowfall, 9) humidity, and 10) global sea level.

Air temperatures over land, over oceans, and in the lower atmosphere are all increasing. The temperature of water at the surface of oceans is increasing, and so is the temperature of water within the top half-mile of oceans. Arctic sea ice, glaciers, and the amount of land covered by snow are all diminishing. Humidity, or the amount of water vapor in the air, is increasing, and the global sea level is rising. All of these indicators point to a changing climate, and one that is consistently warming.

International Panel on Climate Change

The International Panel on Climate Change (IPCC) is a group of scientists from many countries who study and monitor Earth's climate. Scientists use evidence from the past to learn about climate change. Various methods including ice cores, seafloor sediment, fossils, and tree rings help scientists study Earth's climate history and relate it to our climate today.

By studying Earth's past climate, the IPCC has concluded that Earth's climate is growing warmer. According to the IPCC, the reason for this global warming is an increase of carbon dioxide in the atmosphere, resulting from the burning of fossil fuels in power plants, factories, and automobile engines.

© Houghton Mifflin Harcourt Publishing Company

Carbon Dioxide

Currently, human activities release about 21 billion tons of carbon dioxide into the air each year. Research has shown that carbon dioxide pollution in the atmosphere has increased the average temperature of Earth. In the past 100 years, the average temperature in the United States has increased by about 0.7°C. This global warming may not sound like a lot, but it will significantly affect Earth's climate. Changing climate patterns will bring droughts to some areas and floods to others.

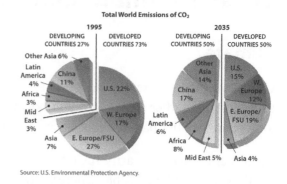

Source: U.S. Environmental Protection Agency.

The effects of global warming could be devastating on a global scale. Some scientists have predicted an increase in global temperature of 2°C to 4°C during this century. An increase of only a few degrees worldwide could melt the polar icecaps and raise sea levels. Many coastal cities would be under water, including cities such as Miami, New Orleans, and Houston.

Climate Change and Deforestation

Deforestation is also a cause of climate change. Forests, like oceans, are carbon sinks. A carbon sink is anything in the environment that absorbs and stores carbon. Plants, including trees, are important because they remove carbon dioxide from the atmosphere during photosynthesis and they store the absorbed carbon as long as they are alive.

Deforestation through burning trees directly releases the stored carbon in trees back to the atmosphere. Not only that, but there will be fewer trees available to capture and store the carbon again through photosynthesis.

Cutting timber can also cause climate change. Not only does the cutting of timber release carbon dioxide into the atmosphere through the burning of fossil fuels for equipment to harvest and process the trees, but the removal of the trees also removes important carbon sinks from the ecosystem.

Natural Causes of Climate Change

As mentioned before, human activities are not the only cause of climate change. For example, sunspots are thought to cause changes to Earth's climate. Sunspots are regions of the Sun's surface that are up to 3,000°C cooler than the surrounding areas. Sunspots appear darker than the surrounding area. The number of sunspots increases and decreases in a cycle that lasts roughly 11 years. Scientists theorize that these changes in sunspot activity may affect Earth's climate. Sunspots are cooler than surrounding areas, but high sunspot activity is associated with an increase in the brightness of the Sun and an increase in the amount of solar energy absorbed by Earth. So, periods of high sunspot activity are associated with warming trends. Periods of low sunspot activity are associated with cooling trends.

Natural events such as volcanic eruptions also can affect climate. The dust from volcanic eruptions can remain in the atmosphere for several years. The debris blocks sunlight from reaching Earth's surface, causing global temperatures to fall. In 1991, Mount Pinatubo in the Philippines erupted, followed shortly afterwards by the eruption of Mount Hudson in Chile. Global temperatures fell about 1°C during the next two years.

© Houghton Mifflin Harcourt Publishing Company

What Is Climate Change?

Write the answers to the questions on the lines below.

1. What is weather? _____

_____

2. What is currently happening to Earth's climate?

_____

3. What is one natural cause of climate change?

_____

4. How is energy from the Sun distributed around the globe?

_____

_____

5. What is a carbon sink?

_____

_____

6. What do scientists think causes global carbon emissions to rise?

_____

_____

7. Currently, how many tons of carbon dioxide are released into the atmosphere each year by human activities?

_____

_____

8. Main Idea What is climate change?

_____

_____

_____

© Houghton Mifflin Harcourt Publishing Company

Earth Science
Core Skills Science, Grade 7

9. **Vocabulary** Describe climate change using the terms *climate* and *global warming*.

_____

_____

_____

10. **Reading Skill: Main Idea and Details** Describe how sunspots might change Earth's climate.

_____

_____

_____

11. **Critical Thinking: Synthesize** Why are scientific predictions concerning climate change important to human society?

_____

_____

_____

12. **Inquiry Skill: Interpret** What do scientists predict will happen to global carbon emissions by 2035?

_____

_____

_____

13. **Test Prep** When levels of carbon dioxide increase in the atmosphere, what happens to the average global temperature?

   A It increases.

   B It decreases.

   C It stays the same.

   D It goes up and then down.

© Houghton Mifflin Harcourt Publishing Company

What Is the Periodic Table?

History of the Periodic Table

All matter is made up of atoms, and all atoms can be identified as a particular element based on the number of protons in the nucleus of the atoms. The elements are organized into a chart called the periodic table of elements. Many scientists over the years have worked to organize the many elements. Dimitri Mendeleev is credited with organizing the first modern periodic table.

Mendeleev began by arranging the elements by increasing atomic mass. However, this arrangement was not perfect. There were many places in the table where elements should have their positions switched to make physical and chemical properties of neighboring elements correspond better. When he organized his periodic table, Mendeleev left spaces for elements that had not yet been discovered, but that could be predicted based on trends in the periodic table.

Henry Moseley further refined Mendeleev's periodic table by organizing the elements by atomic number, not atomic mass. This arrangement is still used today, and the periodic table is a useful model for understanding elements and their relationships.

Information in the Periodic Table

The periodic table consists of one box for each known element. The boxes are arranged based on the elements' physical and chemical properties. Boxes display a variety of information about each element.

Each element has a chemical symbol that is used to represent the element. Chemical symbols can be one, two, or three letters long, and only the first letter is capitalized. The chemical symbol is usually displayed in the middle of the element box.

An atomic number is the number of protons in the nucleus of an element. Every atom of that element has the same, unique number of protons. So, it is the number of protons that identifies an element. The atomic number is usually shown above the chemical symbol in each element box on the periodic table. Many periodic tables are customized to show more information about each element, such as average atomic mass, the typical state of matter of the element, or the electron configuration.

Arrangement of the Periodic Table

The periodic table is arranged from left to right by increasing atomic number. Each horizontal row of elements on the periodic table is called a period. The physical and chemical properties of elements in a row follow a repeating pattern across the period. There are seven periods in the periodic table.

Each vertical column of elements on the periodic table is called a group. Elements in the same group generally have similar chemical and physical properties. This is because elements in the same group have similar electron arrangements and similar reactivity. A group is also known as a family. There are 18 groups in the periodic table, not including the lanthanide and actinide series, which are generally shown below the periodic table to save space.

© Houghton Mifflin Harcourt Publishing Company

Periodic Table of Elements

Alkali metals → Group 1

Alkaline earth metals → Group 2

Halogens → Group 17

Noble gases → Group 18

1																	18
1 **H** 1.008	2											13	14	15	16	17	2 **He** 4.003
3 **Li** 6.941	4 **Be** 9.012											5 **B** 10.81	6 **C** 12.01	7 **N** 14.01	8 **O** 16.00	9 **F** 19.00	10 **Ne** 20.18
11 **Na** 22.99	12 **Mg** 24.31	3	4	5	6	7	8	9	10	11	12	13 **Al** 26.96	14 **Si** 28.09	15 **P** 30.97	16 **S** 32.07	17 **Cl** 35.45	18 **Ar** 39.95
19 **K** 39.10	20 **Ca** 40.08	21 **Sc** 44.96	22 **Ti** 47.86	23 **V** 50.94	24 **Cr** 52.00	25 **Mn** 54.94	26 **Fe** 55.85	27 **Co** 58.93	28 **Ni** 58.96	29 **Cu** 63.55	30 **Zn** 65.41	31 **Ga** 69.72	32 **Ge** 72.61	33 **As** 74.92	34 **Se** 78.95	35 **Br** 79.90	36 **Kr** 83.80
37 **Rb** 85.47	38 **Sr** 87.62	39 **Y** 88.91	40 **Zr** 91.22	41 **Nb** 92.91	42 **Mo** 95.94	43 **Tc** (98)	44 **Ru** 101.1	45 **Rh** 102.9	46 **Pd** 106.4	47 **Ag** 107.9	48 **Cd** 112.4	49 **In** 114.8	50 **Sn** 118.7	51 **Sb** 121.8	52 **Te** 127.6	53 **I** 126.9	54 **Xe** 131.3
55 **Cs** 132.9	56 **Ba** 137.3	57 **La** 138.9	72 **Hf** 178.5	73 **Ta** 180.9	74 **W** 183.9	75 **Re** 186.2	76 **Os** 190.2	77 **Ir** 192.2	78 **Pt** 195.1	79 **Au** 197.0	80 **Hg** 200.6	81 **Tl** 204.4	82 **Pb** 207.2	83 **Bi** 208.9	84 **Po** (209)	85 **At** (210)	86 **Rn** (222)
87 **Fr** (223)	88 **Ra** (226)	89 **Ac** (227)	104 **Rf** (263)	105 **Db** (262)	106 **Sg** (266)	107 **Bh** (267)	108 **Hs** (277)	109 **Mt** (268)	110 **Ds** (281)	111 **Rg** (272)							

Transition elements (groups 3–12)

58 **Ce** 140.11	59 **Pr** 140.90	60 **Nd** 144.24	61 **Pm** (145)	62 **Sm** 150.36	63 **Eu** 151.96	64 **Gd** 157.25	65 **Tb** 158.92	66 **Dy** 162.50	67 **Ho** 164.93	68 **Er** 167.25	69 **Tm** 168.93	70 **Yb** 173.04	71 **Lu** 174.96
90 **Th** 232.03	91 **Pa** 231.03	92 **U** 238.02	93 **Np** (237)	94 **Pu** (244)	95 **AM** (243)	96 **Cm** (247)	97 **Bk** (247)	98 **Cf** (251)	99 **Es** (252)	100 **Fm** (257)	101 **Md** (258)	102 **No** (259)	103 **Lr** (262)

Classification of Elements

Elements can be identified by their physical and chemical properties. For example, elements can be classified as metals, nonmetals, and metalloids, according to their properties. The zigzag line on the periodic table helps indicate which elements are metals, which are nonmetals, and which are metalloids.

Metals are found to the left of the zigzag line on the periodic table. Metals are typically shiny, malleable, and good conductors of heat and electricity. Atoms of most metals have few electrons in their outer energy level. Most metals are solid at room temperature. The most reactive metals are found in the first group of the periodic table. These are elements that easily lose one electron to form chemical bonds.

Nonmetals are found to the right of the zigzag line on the periodic table. Nonmetals are dull and brittle, which means they break easily and cannot be easily shaped like metals. Atoms of most nonmetals have an almost complete set of electrons in their outer level. More than half of the nonmetals are gases at room temperature. The most reactive nonmetals are in group 17. These are the elements that form chemical bonds and gain a single electron to fill their outer energy levels.

Metalloids, also called semiconductors, are the elements that border the zigzag line on the periodic table. Metalloids share the properties of metals and nonmetals. Atoms of metalloids have about half of a complete set of electrons in their outer energy level. Metalloids have some properties of metals and some properties of nonmetals.

86

What Is the Periodic Table?

Fill in the blanks.

1. Elements that are shiny and malleable are classified as _____.

2. The modern periodic table is arranged by _____, not by atomic mass.

3. There are _____ periods in the periodic table.

4. The atomic number of an element is the number of _____ in the nucleus of an atom of that element.

5. Elements that are dull and brittle are classified as _____.

6. Each element has a _____ that is used to represent the element.

7. A group is also known as a _____.

8. **Main Idea** How are elements arranged on the periodic table?

_____

_____

_____

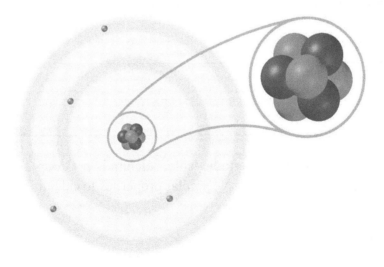

87

Physical Science
Core Skills Science, Grade 7

9. Vocabulary Write a short paragraph using the terms *metal*, *nonmetal*, and *metalloid*.

_____

_____

_____

10. Reading Skill: Compare and Contrast Explain the difference between a group and a period on the periodic table.

_____

_____

_____

11. Critical Thinking: Synthesize How can the zigzag line on the periodic table be used to determine properties of elements?

_____

_____

_____

12. Inquiry Skill: Infer How can the periodic table be used to make inferences about the properties of an element?

_____

_____

_____

13. Test Prep Calcium is a metal. On the periodic table, calcium is in Group 2 and Period 4. Which of the following elements is **most likely** to have similar properties to calcium?

A scandium, Group 3 and Period 4

B potassium, Group 1 and Period 4

C aluminum, Group 13 and Period 3

D magnesium, Group 2 and Period 3

© Houghton Mifflin Harcourt Publishing Company

How Is Mass Conserved in Chemical Reactions?

Chemical Reactions

Chemical reactions are occurring constantly in the world around you. Chemical reactions even occur inside of you. A chemical reaction occurs when one set of substances is changed to a different set of substances. Reactants are substances that come together to react in a chemical reaction. Products are what is produced during a chemical reaction. Atoms are never lost or gained in a chemical reaction. They are just rearranged. Every atom in the reactants becomes part of the products. When writing a chemical equation, the total number of atoms of each element in the reactants should equal the total number of atoms of that element in the products. This process is called balancing the equation.

Law of Conservation of Mass

Balancing equations comes from the work of a French chemist, Antoine Lavoisier. In the 1700s, Lavoisier found that the total mass of the reactants was always the same as the total mass of the products. Lavoisier's work led to the Law of Conservation of Mass. This law states that matter is neither created nor destroyed in chemical and physical changes. This means that the total mass of the reactants is the same as the total mass of the products. Also, because the number of atoms is not changed by the reaction, the total mass of each element is the same in the products as in the reactants. A chemical equation must show the same numbers and kinds of atoms on both sides of the equation's arrow even though the atoms are rearranged.

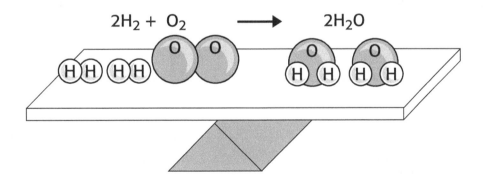

Mole

A mole is a unit of measurement, just like a dozen or a kilogram. It is the amount of a substance containing as many particles as there are atoms in 12 grams of carbon-12. This number is also called Avogadro's number. The mass of one mole of a pure substance is called the molar mass of that substance. Molar mass is usually written in units of g/mol. The molar mass of an element is numerically equal to the atomic mass of the element in atomic mass units. Because of the Law of Conservation of Mass, you can calculate the number of moles of a particular type of atom in the products if you know how many moles of that atom were in the reactants. You can use molar mass to determine the number of grams if you know the number of moles.

© Houghton Mifflin Harcourt Publishing Company

Exothermic and Endothermic Reactions

The amount of energy in chemical reactions is also conserved. Energy that is stored in the form of chemical bonds is called chemical energy. During a chemical change, energy can be absorbed or released as the bonds change. Molecules of hydrocarbons and oxygen have stored chemical energy. When a hydrocarbon burns, the chemical energy changes form, but the total amount of energy of the reactants always equals the total amount of energy of the products and their surroundings. This reaction is an exothermic reaction, a chemical reaction in which energy is released to the surroundings as heat. The released energy comes from the chemical bond energy of the reactants. The energy that is released as the products form is greater than the energy absorbed to break the bonds in the reactants. In all exothermic reactions, the products have less energy than the reactants. Energy is often released as heat, but exothermic reactions can produce other forms of energy, such as light or electrical energy.

If you put hydrated barium hydroxide and ammonium nitrate in a flask, the reaction between them takes so much energy from the surroundings that water in the air will condense and then freeze on the surface of the flask. This reaction is an endothermic reaction, a chemical reaction in which energy is absorbed as heat. More energy is needed to break the bonds in the reactants than is given off by forming bonds in the products. When an endothermic reaction happens, you may be able to notice a drop in temperature. Sometimes, endothermic reactions need more energy than they can get from their surroundings. In those cases, energy must be added to cause the reaction to take place. Usually, the energy is added as heat, but some reactions use other forms of energy. For example, light energy is absorbed during photosynthesis.

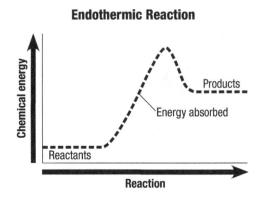

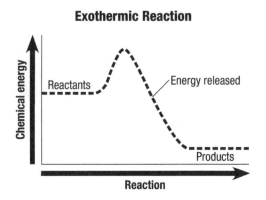

© Houghton Mifflin Harcourt Publishing Company

Name _____ Date _____

How Is Mass Conserved in Chemical Reactions?

Fill in the blanks.

1. A balanced chemical _____ must show the same numbers and kinds of atoms on both sides of the arrow.

2. Mass is never _____ or _____ in an ordinary chemical reaction.

3. _____ come together in a chemical reaction to produce different products.

4. The mass of one _____ of a pure substance is called the molar mass of that substance.

5. Both _____ and _____ are conserved during chemical reactions.

6. The work of the French chemist _____ led to the Law of Conservation of Mass.

7. A _____ occurs when one set of substances is changed to a different set of substances.

8. **Vocabulary** Write a short paragraph using the terms *product*, *reactant*, and *conservation of mass*.

_____

_____

_____

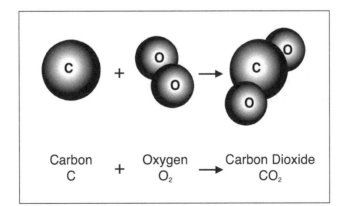

© Houghton Mifflin Harcourt Publishing Company

Physical Science
Core Skills Science, Grade 7

9. **Main Idea** What is the Law of Conservation of Mass?

_____

_____

10. **Reading Skill: Compare and Contrast** What is the difference between an endothermic reaction and an exothermic reaction?

_____

_____

_____

11. **Critical Thinking: Infer** If you know that there are three atoms of oxygen in the products of a chemical reaction, what can you infer about the reactants?

_____

_____

12. **Inquiry Skill: Apply** During a camping trip, you place a large log in the fire. In the morning, the mass of the ashes left in the fire pit is much less than the mass of the log. Why does this observation not show a violation of the Law of Conservation of Mass?

_____

_____

_____

13. **Test Prep** Which chemical equation below correctly shows the conservation of matter?

A $C_5H_{12} + O_2 \rightarrow CO_2 + H_2O$

B $C_5H_{12} + 8O_2 \rightarrow 5CO_2 + 3H_2O$

C $C_5H_{12} + 8O_2 \rightarrow 5CO_2 + 6H_2O$

D $C_5H_{12} + 16O_2 \rightarrow 3CO_2 + 4H_2O$

© Houghton Mifflin Harcourt Publishing Company

What Is Nuclear Fusion?

Energy and the Sun

Earth is made up of many connected, dynamic systems that require energy to continue functioning. Most of the energy that drives Earth's systems is heat released by nuclear reactions. Some of this heat is generated internally, deep inside the planet. Other energy enters Earth's systems from an external source, the sun. Solar radiation warms Earth's atmosphere and surface. All of the energy that reaches Earth from the sun is produced by nuclear fusion, a kind of nuclear reaction. During nuclear fusion, the nuclei of hydrogen atoms combine to form larger nuclei of helium. This process releases energy. Fusion reactions occur only at temperatures of more than 15,000,000°C. These conditions are difficult to achieve in science laboratories, so fusion is not a major energy source on Earth.

Solar Fusion

The sun contains traces of almost all chemical elements, but about 99% of the sun's mass is made up of hydrogen and helium. In the sun's core, nuclei of hydrogen atoms fuse to form helium atoms. This process, called nuclear fusion, converts mass into huge amounts of energy, which gives the sun its high temperature and brightness. The sun changes more than 600 million tons of hydrogen into helium every second. Yet this amount of hydrogen is small compared with the total mass of hydrogen in the sun. The heat and energy from solar fusion transfer through the layers of the sun by radiation and convection.

The Process of Nuclear Fusion

Nuclei of hydrogen atoms are the primary fuel for solar nuclear fusion. A hydrogen atom, the simplest of all atoms, commonly consists of only one electron and one proton. Inside the sun, however, electrons are stripped from the protons by the sun's intense heat. Some of these protons are converted to neutrons when the proton emits a particle called a positron. This also produces energy. In a series of steps, two protons and two neutrons combine to form a helium nucleus. The helium nucleus has about 0.7% less mass than the hydrogen nuclei that combined to form it. The difference in mass is converted into energy during the series of fusion reactions that form helium. The energy released during nuclear fusion causes the sun to emit light and gives the sun its high temperature.

© Houghton Mifflin Harcourt Publishing Company

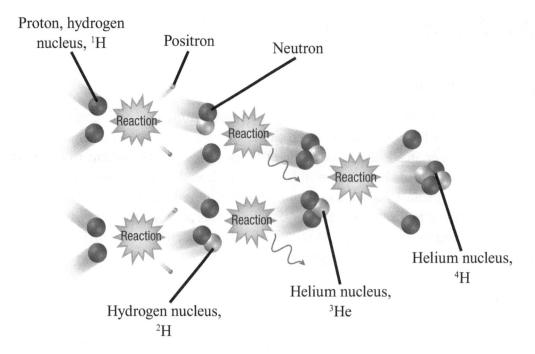

Solar Fusion

Nuclear Fission

Another type of nuclear reaction is nuclear fission, which is the energy source of nuclear power plants. During nuclear fission, the nucleus of atoms is split into two or more nuclei. Taken together, the mass of these nuclei is slightly less than the mass of the original nucleus, and a very large amount of energy is released. In addition, a released neutron can cause another nucleus to split. One reaction triggers another fission reaction, causing a nuclear chain reaction.

Mass-Energy Equivalence

Einstein's $E_R = mc^2$ is one of the most famous equations of the twentieth century and is known as the mass-energy equivalence. This equation shows that an object has a certain amount of energy (E_R), known as rest energy, simply by virtue of its mass. The rest energy of a body is equal to its mass, m, multiplied by the speed of light squared, c^2. Thus, the mass of a body is a measure of its rest energy. This equation is significant because rest energy is an aspect of special relativity that was not predicted by classical physics. Nuclear reactions utilize this relationship by converting mass, or rest energy, into other forms of energy.

© Houghton Mifflin Harcourt Publishing Company

What Is Nuclear Fusion?

Fill in the blanks.

1. During nuclear _____, two light nuclei combine to form a heavier nucleus.

2. During nuclear _____, energy is released as the nucleus of a large atom breaks apart to form two smaller nuclei.

3. The sun produces energy by turning _____ into helium.

4. Nuclear reactions convert _____ into other forms of energy.

5. A nuclear _____ reaction can occur during nuclear fission, as free neutrons are continually released.

6. Nuclear fusion takes place in the sun's _____.

7. **Main Idea** Describe why nuclear fusion is important to life on Earth.

   _____

   _____

   _____

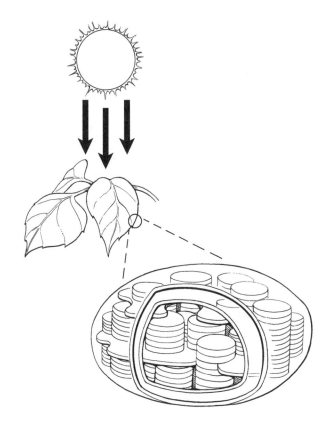

© Houghton Mifflin Harcourt Publishing Company

8. Vocabulary Explain solar fusion using the terms *hydrogen*, *helium*, and *nuclear fusion*.

_____

_____

_____

9. Reading Skill: Compare and Contrast Explain the difference and similarity between nuclear fusion and nuclear fission.

_____

_____

_____

10. Critical Thinking: Synthesize The sun creates energy by a process of turning hydrogen into helium. Why don't we fuse hydrogen to create energy on Earth?

_____

_____

_____

11. Inquiry Skill: Use Models Label the nuclear fusion model shown below.

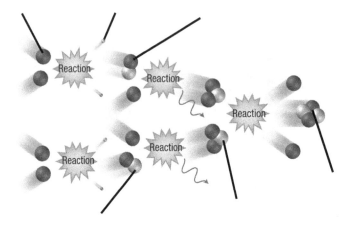

12. Test Prep What is the source of energy emitted by the sun?

   A nuclear fusion

   B nuclear fission

   C nuclear radiation

   D nuclear chain reaction

96

What Are Newton's Laws of Motion?

Sir Isaac Newton

Sir Isaac Newton (1642-1727) was an English scientist and mathematician who studied a variety of subjects, including mathematics, physics, optics, astronomy, and even alchemy. Newton is well known for publishing the *Principia*, a multi-edition book which outlined his laws of motion. The ideas in the *Principia* had a profound effect on the way scientists viewed physics, astronomy, and gravity.

Forces

A force is simply a push or a pull. When the wind pushes a sailboat, a force is being applied. When a locomotive engine pulls rail cars, a force is being applied. Force is measured in a unit called the newton (N). All of the forces acting on an object can be added up to calculate the net force.

All forces have two properties: direction and magnitude. All forces act on objects. For any push to occur, something has to receive the push. The same is true for any pull. Your fingers exert forces to pull open books or to push the keys on a computer. Therefore, the forces act on the books and keys. A force can change the velocity of an object. This change in velocity can be a change in speed, direction, or both. In other words, forces can cause acceleration.

Newton's First Law of Motion

In the 1630s, Galileo concluded correctly that it is an object's nature to maintain its state of motion or rest. Note that an object on which no force is acting is not necessarily at rest; the object could also be moving with a constant velocity. This concept was further developed by Newton in 1687 and has come to be known as Newton's first law of motion.

Newton's first law of motion states that an object at rest remains at rest and an object in motion maintains the same speed and direction of travel unless an unbalanced force acts on the object. Inertia is the property of an object that resists a change to speed or direction of motion. So, Newton's first law is also called the law of inertia.

When the forces on an object produce a net force of 0 N, the forces are balanced. Balanced forces will not cause a change in the motion of a moving object, and balanced forces do not cause a nonmoving object to start moving.

When the net force on an object is not 0 N, the forces on the object are unbalanced. Unbalanced forces produce a change in motion, such as a change in speed or a change in direction. Unbalanced forces are necessary to cause a nonmoving object to start moving. Unbalanced forces are also necessary to change the motion of moving objects.

© Houghton Mifflin Harcourt Publishing Company

Newton's Second Law of Motion

Newton's second law of motion, also known as the law of acceleration, describes the motion of an object when an unbalanced force acts on the object. Acceleration is the rate at which speed or direction of motion of an object changes. According to Newton's second law, for a given force, the acceleration of an object decreases as its mass increases and its acceleration increases as its mass decreases. Also, an object's acceleration increases as the force on the object increases and an object's acceleration decreases as the force on the object decreases. The figure below shows the relationship between mass and acceleration.

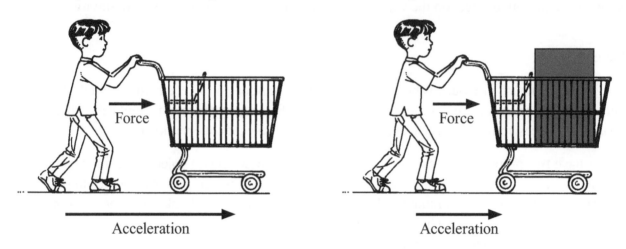

The acceleration of an object is always in the same direction as the force applied. The relationship of acceleration (*a*) to mass (*m*) and force (*F*) can be expressed mathematically with the following equation:

$$F = m \times a$$

Newton's Third Law

A force is exerted on an object when that object interacts with another object in its environment. Newton recognized that a single isolated force cannot exist. Instead, forces always exist in pairs.

Newton's third law states that all forces act in pairs. If a force is exerted, another force occurs that is equal in size and opposite in direction. For example, when a frog jumps, its legs exert a force on the ground. This is the action force. The ground also exerts an equal force on the frog's legs. This is the reaction force, and it is in the opposite direction as the action force. The force from the ground to the frog's legs causes the frog to move!

Can you think of other examples of Newton's third law? One that you might not think of is the relationship between Earth and the Sun. The force that the sun exerts on Earth is equal and opposite to the force that Earth exerts on the sun. This relationship is an example of Newton's third law of motion.

A force is always exerted by one object on another object. This rule is true for all forces, including action and reaction forces. However, action and reaction forces in pairs do not act on the same object. If they did, the net force would always be 0 N and nothing would ever move!

© Houghton Mifflin Harcourt Publishing Company

Physical Science
Core Skills Science, Grade 7

What Are Newton's Laws of Motion?

Fill in the blanks.

1. For every action force there is a(n) _____ force that is equal in magnitude, but opposite in direction.

2. Force is equal to _____ times acceleration.

3. The rate at which speed or direction of motion changes is _____.

4. Newton's _____ law of motion explains that forces act in pairs.

5. The English physicist _____ developed three laws that explained the relationships between force and motion.

6. A(n) _____ force will cause a change in direction or speed or both.

7. A(n) _____ is a push or a pull.

8. **Main Idea** What are Newton's Laws of Motion?

   _____

   _____

   _____

9. **Vocabulary** Write a paragraph using the terms *force*, *balanced forces*, *unbalanced forces*, and *net force*.

   _____

   _____

   _____

   _____

10. **Reading Skill: Main Idea and Details** What causes a change in speed, in direction of motion, or both?

    _____

    _____

    _____

© Houghton Mifflin Harcourt Publishing Company

Physical Science
Core Skills Science, Grade 7

11. Critical Thinking: Analyze Use Newton's second law of motion to describe how to increase the acceleration of an object that is pushed by a force.

_____

_____

_____

_____

12. Inquiry Skill: Use Models and Infer When a soccer ball is kicked, action and reaction forces are exerted. Draw a diagram to model the action and reaction forces between the foot and the ball.

Why don't the action and reaction forces cancel each other out when a soccer ball is kicked?

_____

_____

13. Test Prep Which of the following may happen when a moving object experiences balanced forces?

    A The object starts to move.

    B The object changes speed.

    C The object changes direction.

    D The object retains its velocity.

© Houghton Mifflin Harcourt Publishing Company

What Are Electromagnetic Forces?

Fundamental Forces

A force is a push or a pull on an object. Scientists identify four fundamental forces in nature. These forces are gravity, the electromagnetic force, the strong nuclear force, and the weak nuclear force. The fundamental forces vary widely in strength and the distance over which they act.

The strong nuclear force holds together the protons and neutrons in the nuclei of atoms and is the strongest of all the forces. However, it is negligible over distances greater than the size of an atomic nucleus. Within the nucleus though, this force is strong enough to keep protons bound tightly together by overcoming their electrical repulsions. The weak nuclear force acts over even smaller distances, about the diameter of a proton. It is about one-millionth as strong as the strong force. The weak force is important because it is involved in the nuclear decay of atoms. It is also important in the nuclear reactions that provide heat and light from the sun.

The gravitational and electromagnetic forces act over longer distances. Their effect extends an infinite distance, although these effects decrease rapidly as distance between objects increases. The electromagnetic force is about 1/100 the strength of the strong nuclear force. The gravitational force, the weakest of the four forces, is much weaker than the electromagnetic force. Consider a proton and an electron in an atom. The electromagnetic force is about 1040 times as great as the gravitational force between them! That is why the effects of the electromagnetic force can be observed in the interaction of atoms while the gravitational force can be observed only in the interactions of very large objects.

Electric Force

The electric force is a universal force that exists between any two charged objects. Opposite charges attract while like charges repel. Electric force does not require that objects touch. How do charges interact over a distance? One way to model this property of charges is with the concept of an electric field. An electric field always exists in the space around a charged particle. Any other charged particle in that field will experience an electric force. This force is the result of the electric field associated with the first charged particle.

The electric force between two charged objects varies depending on the amount of charge on each object and the distance between them. The electric force between two objects is proportional to the product of the charges on the objects. If the charge on one object is doubled, the electric force between the objects will also be doubled, as long as the distance between the objects remains the same. The electric force is also inversely proportional to the square of the distance between two objects. For example, if the distance between two charges is doubled, the electric force between them decreases to one-fourth its original value. If the distance between two small charges is quadrupled, the electric force between them decreases to one-sixteenth its original value.

© Houghton Mifflin Harcourt Publishing Company

Magnetic Force

Any object that produces a magnetic field is considered a magnet. Permanent magnets and electromagnets are used in many everyday and scientific applications. Huge electromagnets are used to pick up and move heavy loads, such as scrap iron at a recycling plant. All types of magnets attract iron-containing objects such as paper clips and nails. Iron objects are most strongly attracted to the ends of such a magnet. These ends are called poles; one is called the north pole, and the other is called the south pole. If a bar magnet is suspended from its midpoint so that it can swing freely in a horizontal plane, it will rotate until its north pole points north and its south pole points south. Magnets are also used in meters, motors, and loudspeakers. Magnetic tapes are routinely used in sound- and video-recording equipment, and magnetic recording material is used on computer disks.

Electromagnetic Forces

Electricity and magnetism are related forces. When a compass is held close to a wire with an electric charge flowing through it, the compass needle no longer points north because an electric current produces a magnetic field. A compass needle is a magnet. It moves from its north-south orientation only when it is in a magnetic field different from Earth's. The motion of electrons in the wire produces a magnetic field around the wire.

A single loop of wire carrying a current does not have a very strong magnetic field, but if you make a number of parallel loops, they will combine to make a much stronger field. A solenoid is a coil of wire that produces a magnetic field when carrying an electric current. The magnetic field around a solenoid is very similar to the magnetic field of a bar magnet. The strength of the magnetic field of a solenoid increases as more loops per meter are used. The magnetic field also becomes stronger as the current in the wire is increased.

An electromagnet is made up of a solenoid wrapped around an iron core. The magnetic field of the solenoid makes the domains inside the iron core line up. The magnetic field of the electromagnet is the field of the solenoid plus the field of the magnetized core. As a result, the magnetic field of an electromagnet may be hundreds of times stronger than the magnetic field of just the solenoid. To make an electromagnet stronger, you can increase the number of loops per meter in the solenoid. You can also increase the electric current in the wire. Some electromagnets are strong enough to lift a car or levitate a train.

When a magnet is in motion relative to a wire, the opposite effect occurs. The magnetic field causes charged particles to move inside a conductor, such as a copper wire. However, this occurs only when the magnet is moving or when the conductor is moving. It is the relative motion of wire and the magnetic field that causes electrons to move, and it is this motion that generates an electric current. The process by which an electric current is made by changing a magnetic field is called electromagnetic induction.

An electric generator in a power plant uses electromagnetic induction to change mechanical energy into electrical energy. The energy that generators convert into electrical energy comes from different sources. The source in nuclear power plants is thermal energy from a nuclear reaction. The energy boils water into steam. The steam turns a turbine. The turbine turns the magnet of the generator, which induces an electric current and generates electrical energy. Other kinds of power plants burn fuel such as coal or gas to release thermal energy. Hydroelectric plants use the energy of falling water to turn a turbine.

© Houghton Mifflin Harcourt Publishing Company

What Are Electromagnetic Forces?

Write the answers to the questions on the lines below.

1. What keeps the protons in an atomic nucleus from flying away from one another?

_____

2. Which is the weakest of the four fundamental forces?

_____

3. What is electromagnetic induction?

_____

_____

4. What is the electric force?

_____

_____

5. What is an electromagnet?

_____

_____

6. What does the electric force between two objects depend upon?

_____

_____

7. What is a solenoid?

_____

8. **Main Idea** What are electromagnetic forces?

_____

_____

_____

© Houghton Mifflin Harcourt Publishing Company

9. **Vocabulary** Write a paragraph describing electromagnetic forces using the terms *force*, *solenoid*, and *electromagnet*.

_____

_____

_____

10. **Reading Skill: Main Idea and Details** How do electric power plants generate a current?

_____

_____

11. **Critical Thinking: Analyze** Which will produce the strongest magnetic field, an electric current of 1 ampere or an electric current of 1000 amperes?

_____

_____

_____

12. **Inquiry Skill: Infer** What happens to an electromagnet when the current is turned off?

_____

_____

_____

13. **Test Prep** A current-carrying wire is wrapped in a coil as shown. What do the thin lines with arrow heads in the drawing represent?

   A The electric field around the wire.

   B The magnetic field around the wire.

   C The path of the electrons around the wire.

   D The potential difference around the wire.

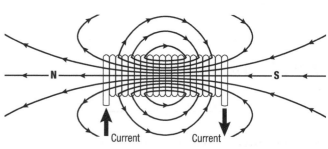

14. Which of the following changes will increase the strength of a solenoid?

   A add coils

   B remove coils

   C decrease the current

   D reverse the current

© Houghton Mifflin Harcourt Publishing Company

What Is Kinetic Energy?

Energy

Energy is the ability to do work. Work is done when a force causes an object to move in the direction of the force. When one object does work on another, energy is transferred from the first object to the second object. This energy allows the second object to do work. There are many types of energy. Energy can be converted from one form to another, but it is never created or destroyed. This is the Law of Conservation of Energy.

Kinetic Energy

Kinetic energy is the energy of motion. All moving objects have kinetic energy. Kinetic energy depends on speed and mass. Like all forms of energy, kinetic energy can be used to do work. The faster something is moving, the more kinetic energy it has. Also, the greater the mass of a moving object, the greater its kinetic energy is. In equation form, kinetic energy is $KE = \frac{1}{2}(mv^2)$, which is stated as "kinetic energy equals mass times velocity (speed) squared multiplied by half."

Potential Energy and Mechanical Energy

Potential energy is stored energy. Potential energy is the energy an object has because of its position. For example, a stretched bow has potential energy because work has been done to change its shape. The energy of that work is turned into potential energy. Chemical energy, electrical energy, and nuclear energy can all be considered forms of potential energy because the energy is stored in particles of matter.

Mechanical energy is the total energy of motion and position of an object. Both potential and kinetic energy are kinds of mechanical energy. Mechanical energy can be all potential energy, all kinetic energy, or some of each. The mechanical energy of an object remains the same unless it transfers some of its energy to another object. But even if the mechanical energy of an object stays the same, the potential energy or kinetic energy it has can increase or decrease.

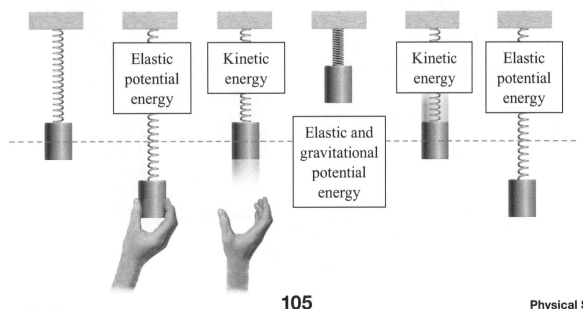

105

© Houghton Mifflin Harcourt Publishing Company

Other Types of Energy

Thermal energy is all of the kinetic energy due to the random motion of the particles that make up an object. Thermal energy also depends on the number of particles. Water in the form of steam has a higher temperature than water in a lake does. But the lake has more thermal energy because the lake has more water particles.

Chemical energy is the energy of a compound that changes as its atoms are rearranged. Chemical energy is a form of potential energy because it depends on the position and arrangement of the atoms in a compound.

Electrical energy is the energy of moving electrons. The electrical energy used in your home comes from power plants. Huge generators turn magnets inside loops of wire. The changing position of a magnet makes electrical energy run through the wire and along the wires from the power plants to electrical way stations to your home. This electrical energy is stored as potential energy until you use it to run your electrical appliances.

Sound energy is caused by an object's vibrations. When you stretch a guitar string, the string stores potential energy. When you let the string go, this potential energy is turned into kinetic energy, which makes the string vibrate. The string also transmits some of this kinetic energy to the air around it. The air particles also vibrate and transmit this energy to your ear. When the sound energy reaches your ear, you hear the sound of the guitar.

Light energy is produced by the vibrations of electrically charged particles. Like sound vibrations, light vibrations cause energy to be transmitted. But the vibrations that transmit light energy don't need to be carried through matter. In fact, light energy can move through a vacuum (an area where there is no matter).

© Houghton Mifflin Harcourt Publishing Company

What Is Kinetic Energy?

Match each definition to its term.

Definitions   **Terms**

_____ 1. energy caused by an object's vibrations

_____ 2. energy of motion

_____ 3. energy produced by the vibrations of electrically charged particles

_____ 4. energy due to position

_____ 5. energy of moving electrons

_____ 6. total energy of motion and position of an object

_____ 7. energy of a compound that changes as atoms are rearranged

_____ 8. kinetic energy due to random motion of particles in an object

a. sound energy

b. thermal energy

c. chemical energy

d. potential energy

e. kinetic energy

f. electrical energy

g. light energy

h. mechanical energy

9. Main Idea What is energy and how is it conserved?

_____

_____

_____

_____

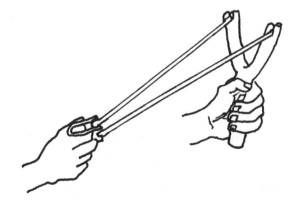

© Houghton Mifflin Harcourt Publishing Company

10. Vocabulary Write a paragraph explaining the energy of motion and the energy of position using the terms *kinetic energy*, *potential energy*, and *mechanical energy*.

_____

_____

_____

11. Reading Skill: Main Idea and Details What properties of an object does kinetic energy depend on?

_____

_____

12. Critical Thinking: Analyze Sam studied kinetic and potential energy by observing apples on a tree during a field investigation. Explain what type of energy these apples have.

_____

_____

_____

13. Inquiry Skill: Use Models Draw a diagram that models an object with kinetic energy, an object with potential energy, and an object with both kinetic energy and potential energy.

14. Test Prep What energy transfer happens when you plug in a blender?

   A Electrical energy becomes light energy and sound energy.

   B Electrical energy becomes kinetic energy and sound energy.

   C Chemical energy becomes light energy and thermal energy.

   D Chemical energy becomes electrical energy.

© Houghton Mifflin Harcourt Publishing Company

What Is Conservation of Energy?

Law of Conservation of Energy

Energy has many forms and can be found almost everywhere. The Law of Conservation of Energy states that energy cannot be created or destroyed. In other words, the total amount of energy in the universe never changes, although energy may change from one form to another. In equation form this law can be expressed as $ME_i = ME_f$.

The Law of Conservation of Energy was developed based on many observations over a long period of time. It is a scientific law because it describes something that always occurs in nature. It is not a theory, however, because it does not explain why energy is conserved.

Although energy and mass are distinct quantities under normal conditions, nuclear reactions can cause a conversion between energy and mass. A small amount of mass can be converted to a large amount of energy, or a large amount of energy can be converted to a small amount of mass. In these cases, it may appear that the laws of conservation are violated. The total amount of mass and equivalent energy is still conserved, however, even though one is converted into the other.

Energy in Systems

Accounting for all of the energy in a given case can be complicated. To make studying a case easier, scientists often limit their view to a small area or a small number of objects. These boundaries define a system.

A system in which energy and matter are exchanged with the surroundings is an open system. If energy but not matter is exchanged, the system is closed. An isolated system is one in which neither energy nor matter is exchanged. Imagine a beaker of water over a burner. If you considered only the flow of energy as the water was heated, it might seem like a closed system. But matter in the form of water vapor leaves the beaker, especially if the water is boiling. Thus, it is an open system. Whenever the total energy in a system increases, the increase must be due to energy that enters the system from an outside source. At the same time, energy is decreased in that source.

Very few real-world systems are isolated systems. Most systems are open. Earth itself might be considered a closed system because its limited exchange of matter with outer space could be ignored. However, Earth receives energy from the sun that is reradiated to space. Therefore, Earth is not an isolated system.

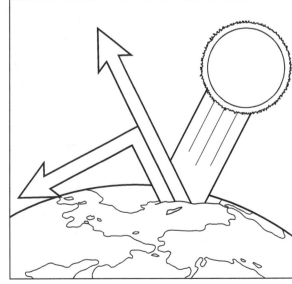

© Houghton Mifflin Harcourt Publishing Company

Energy Conversions

According to the Law of Conservation of Energy, energy cannot be created or destroyed. The total amount of energy in a closed system is always the same. Energy can change from one form to another, but all of the different forms of energy in a system always add up to the same total amount of energy.

An energy conversion is a change from one form of energy to another. Any form of energy can change into any other form of energy. For example, kinetic energy can change into potential energy, and vice versa. Chemical energy in food can be converted into energy that your body can use, and chemical energy in fuels can be converted into thermal energy by burning the fuels. Plants convert light energy into chemical energy during photosynthesis.

When you operate a lawn mower, for example, energy changes to a different form but energy is also conserved. The mower needs gasoline to run. Gasoline has stored energy that is released when it is burned. When the stored energy is considered, the energy present before you start the lawn mower is equal to the energy that is produced. Some of the energy from the gasoline is transferred to the surroundings as heat, which is why the lawn mower gets hot. The total amount of energy released by the gasoline is equal to the energy used to power the lawn mower plus the energy transferred to the surroundings as heat.

Other Conserved Quantities

Matter, energy, and momentum are conserved quantities. That means that none of them is created or destroyed under normal conditions. The Law of Conservation of Matter, which is based on observations of many chemical reactions, states that matter is neither created nor destroyed during a chemical reaction. Therefore, the mass of a system remains constant during any chemical process. The Law of Conservation of Momentum states that the total momentum of two or more objects after a collision is the same as it was before the collision. Anytime two or more objects interact, they may exchange momentum, but the total momentum of a system always stays the same.

© Houghton Mifflin Harcourt Publishing Company

Name _____ Date _____

What Is Conservation of Energy?

Fill in the blanks.

1. Nuclear reactions can cause a conversion between _____ and

   _____.

2. _____, _____, and _____ are
   conserved quantities.

3. An energy _____ is a change from one form of energy to another.

4. A system in which energy and matter are exchanged with the surroundings is a(n)

   _____ system.

5. Conservation of Energy is explained as a scientific law and not a _____
   because it does not explain why energy is conserved.

6. According to the Law of Conservation of Energy, energy cannot be _____ or

   _____ in ordinary chemical changes.

7. A(n) _____ system is one in which neither energy nor matter is exchanged.

8. **Main Idea** What is the Law of Conservation of Energy?

   _____

   _____

   _____

   _____

111

9. **Vocabulary** Write a paragraph about the energy of systems using the terms *open system*, *closed system*, and *isolated system*.

_____

_____

_____

_____

10. **Reading Skill: Apply** List 3 other reactions or systems you encounter on a daily basis and explain how they demonstrate the Law of Conservation of Energy.

_____

_____

_____

_____

11. **Critical Thinking: Synthesize** How does the Law of Conservation of Energy apply to the sun-Earth system?

_____

_____

_____

_____

12. **Inquiry Skill: Infer** Why is it important to know whether a system you are studying is open, closed, or isolated?

_____

_____

_____

_____

13. **Test Prep** As a roller coaster moves down a hill, potential energy is converted into kinetic energy, thermal energy, and sound energy. What is true about the total energy of this system?

   A Energy is lost as the roller coaster moves.

   B Energy is gained as the roller coaster moves.

   C The total energy remains the same as the roller coaster moves.

   D The total energy constantly changes as the roller coaster moves.

© Houghton Mifflin Harcourt Publishing Company

What Are Sound Waves?

Mechanical Waves

Waves transmit energy from one place to another and can interact with objects. Waves transfer energy as they travel, and waves can do work. Waves of almost every kind require a material medium in which to travel. Sound waves cannot travel through outer space because space is very nearly a vacuum. In order for sound waves to travel, they must have a medium such as air or water. Waves that require a material medium are called mechanical waves. Not all wave propagation requires a medium. Electromagnetic waves, such as visible light, radio waves, microwaves, and X-rays, can travel through a vacuum.

Mechanical waves carry energy from one place to another through the vibration of the particles of the medium. Types of mechanical waves include sound waves, ocean waves, which move through water, waves that are carried on guitar and cello strings when they vibrate, and seismic waves that travel through Earth.

Properties of Waves

When the particles of the medium vibrate parallel to the direction of wave motion, the wave is called a longitudinal wave. Sound waves in the air are longitudinal waves because air particles vibrate back and forth in a direction parallel to the direction of wave motion. A wave in which the particles of the disturbed medium move perpendicularly to the wave motion is called a transverse wave.

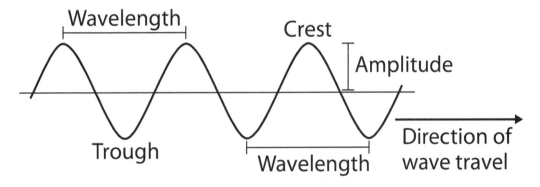

The amount of energy carried by a wave is related to its frequency (the number of waves in a period of time) and to the wavelength (distance from crest to crest of the wave). For a particular type of wave, an increase in frequency increases the amount of energy that the wave carries. Since an increase in the frequency of waves also means a decrease in the wavelength of waves (less distance between any point on a wave and the corresponding point on the next wave, therefore shorter waves), you can see that the shorter the wave, the more energy it carries. The speed of a mechanical wave is constant for any given medium. The wave speed (v) is the frequency of the wave (f) times the wavelength (λ). In equation form, $v = f\lambda$. The speed of a wave changes only when the wave moves from one medium to another or when certain properties of the medium (such as temperature) are varied.

© Houghton Mifflin Harcourt Publishing Company

Physical Science
Core Skills Science, Grade 7

The wavelength of a wave is the distance between any two crests or compressions next to each other in a wave. The distance between two troughs or rarefactions next to each other is also equal to one wavelength. The wavelength can be measured from any point on a wave to the corresponding point on the next wave. A wave with a shorter wavelength carries more energy than a wave with a longer wavelength if they have the same amplitude.

The number of waves produced in a given amount of time is the frequency of the wave. Frequency is usually expressed in hertz (Hz). One hertz equals one wave per second. If the amplitudes are equal, higher frequency waves carry more energy than low-frequency waves.

The amplitude of a wave is related to its height. For a mechanical wave, the amplitude is the maximum distance that the particles of a medium vibrate from their rest position. The larger the amplitude, the taller the wave. A wave with a larger amplitude carries more energy than a wave with a smaller amplitude.

Sound Waves

Sound waves are one type of mechanical wave. Sound energy travels by the vibration of particles in liquids, solids, and gases. If there are no particles to vibrate, no sound is possible. If you put an alarm clock inside a jar and remove all the air from the jar to create a vacuum, you will not be able to hear the alarm.

Resonance of sound waves can occur when one object or system vibrates near the same natural frequency of vibration of a second object or system. This can cause the second object or system to begin vibrating at the natural frequency, which results in a large amplitude of vibration. Examples of resonance include a standing wave on a guitar string and standing sound waves in organ pipes.

© Houghton Mifflin Harcourt Publishing Company

What Are Sound Waves?

Answer questions 1-3 based on the following illustration of a wave with a frequency of 33.3 Hz.

1. What is the amplitude of the wave?

   A 5.0 cm

   B 6.0 cm

   C 10.0 cm

   D 12.0 cm

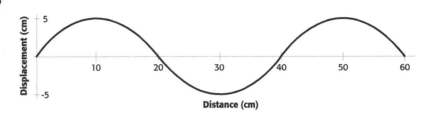

2. What is the speed of the wave?

   A 1.67m/s

   B 6.66 m/s

   C 13.32 m/s

   D 19.98 m/s

3. What is the wavelength of the wave?

   A 5.0 cm

   B 20.0 cm

   C 40.0 cm

   D 60.0 cm

Fill in the blanks.

4. Vibrations in a _____ wave are always parallel to the direction of wave

   motion, while vibrations in a _____ wave are perpendicular to the direction
   of the wave motion.

5. A phenomenon called _____ occurs when one object vibrating at the natural
   frequency of the second object can force the second object to begin vibrating at the same frequency.

6. _____ waves require a material medium to transfer energy.

7. The number of waves produced in a given amount of time is the _____ of
   the wave.

8. **Main Idea** How are sound waves and mechanical waves related?

   _____

   _____

   _____

© Houghton Mifflin Harcourt Publishing Company

9. **Vocabulary** Write a paragraph explaining the properties of waves using the terms *wavelength*, *frequency*, *amplitude*, and *speed*.

_____

_____

_____

_____

10. **Reading Skill: Contrast** What is the difference between electromagnetic waves and mechanical waves?

_____

_____

_____

11. **Critical Thinking: Analyze** Why does a wave with a larger amplitude carry more energy than a wave with a smaller amplitude?

_____

_____

_____

12. **Inquiry Skill: Use Numbers** A wave of frequency 42.5 Hz travels at a speed of 3.5 m/s. What is the wavelength of the wave in centimeters?

13. **Test Prep** Which of the following is a true statement about the energy of a wave?

   A A wave with a shorter wavelength carries more energy than a wave with a longer wavelength if they have the same amplitude.

   B A wave with a smaller amplitude carries more energy than a wave with a larger amplitude.

   C A wave with a longer wavelength carries more energy than a wave with a shorter wavelength if they have the same amplitude.

   D If the amplitudes are equal, lower frequency waves carry more energy than high frequency waves.

© Houghton Mifflin Harcourt Publishing Company

How Does Light Interact With Objects?

The Electromagnetic Spectrum

Some waves can transfer energy without going through a medium. Visible light is one example. Other examples include microwaves made by microwave ovens, TV and radio signals, and X-rays used by dentists and doctors. These waves are electromagnetic waves (EM waves).

In classical electromagnetic wave theory, light is considered to be a wave composed of oscillating electric and magnetic fields. These fields are perpendicular to the direction in which the wave moves. Therefore, electromagnetic waves are transverse waves. The electric and magnetic fields are also at right angles to each other. Although electromagnetic waves do not need a medium, they can go through matter, such as air, water, and glass.

The entire range of EM waves is called the electromagnetic spectrum. It is divided into regions according to the length of the waves. The greater the frequency of an electromagnetic wave, the more energy it transmits.

James Maxwell discovered in 1873 that light was a form of electromagnetic wave. However, the results of some later experiments could not be explained by the wave model of the nature of light. Albert Einstein resolved this conflict in his 1905 paper, for which he received the Nobel Prize in 1921. Einstein assumed that an electromagnetic wave can also be viewed as a stream of particles, now called photons. These results helped form the concept of wave-particle duality, in which all forms of electromagnetic radiation can be described from two points of view. Light and other electromagnetic radiation can behave both like a wave and like a particle; some experiments reveal its wave nature, and other experiments display its particle nature.

Interactions of Light

When waves are moving through a continuous medium or through space, they may move in straight lines like waves on the ocean, spread out in circles like ripples on a pond, or spread out in spheres like sound waves in air. But what happens when a wave meets an object? And what happens when a wave passes into another medium?

Light traveling through a uniform substance, whether it is air, water, or a vacuum, always travels in a straight line. However, when the light encounters a different substance, its path will change. If a material is opaque to the light, part of the light is absorbed and the rest of it is deflected at the surface. This change in the direction of the light is called reflection. If a straight line is drawn perpendicular to the reflecting surface at the point where the incoming ray strikes the surface, the angle of incidence and angle of reflection can be defined with respect to the line called the normal. Careful measurements of the incident and reflected angles reveal that the angles are equal.

© Houghton Mifflin Harcourt Publishing Company

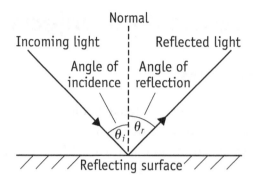

The bending of light as it travels from one medium to another is called refraction. All waves are refracted when they pass from one medium to another at an angle. If light travels from one transparent medium to another at any angle other than straight on (normal to the surface), the light ray changes direction when it meets the boundary. The angles of the incoming and refracted rays are measured with respect to the normal.

When waves pass the edge of an object, they spread out as if a new wave were created there. The same effect occurs when waves pass through an opening, such as an open window or a door. In effect, the waves bend around an object or opening. This bending of waves as they pass an edge is called diffraction. Examples of diffraction include ocean waves bending around jetties and compact discs dispersing light into colors.

Interference is a phenomenon that takes place only between waves of the same or nearly the same wavelength. When several waves are in the same location, they combine to produce a single, new wave that is different from the original waves. This interaction is called interference.

Doppler Effect

Light at the blue end of the spectrum has the shortest wavelengths and the highest frequencies. Light at the red end of the spectrum has the longest wavelengths and the lowest frequencies. The relative motion between a wave source and an observer creates an apparent frequency shift known as the Doppler effect. For example, when a light source is moving away from an observer, the observed frequency will be lower and the wavelength will have stretched out as it is shifted toward the red end of the spectrum. This phenomenon is called red shift. Conversely, if the light source is moving toward the observer, the observed frequency will be higher and the wavelength will be shorter as it is shifted toward the blue end of the spectrum. This is called blue shift.

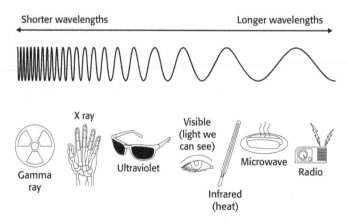

© Houghton Mifflin Harcourt Publishing Company

How Does Light Interact with Objects?

Write the answers to the questions on the lines below.

1. What happens when light waves bounce off an object?

   _____

2. Why is visible light refracted as it travels from air to water?

   _____

   _____

   _____

3. Why are electromagnetic (EM) waves different from other kinds of waves?

   _____

   _____

4. What is transmitted by a light wave?

   _____

5. What is the Doppler effect?

   _____

   _____

6. List the two types of fields that make up electromagnetic waves.

   _____

7. What is interference?

   _____

   _____

8. **Main Idea** What is the electromagnetic spectrum?

   _____

   _____

   _____

119

Physical Science
Core Skills Science, Grade 7

9. **Vocabulary** Write a paragraph explaining the interaction of light with objects using the terms *reflection*, *refraction*, and *diffraction*.

_____

_____

_____

10. **Reading Skill: Main Idea and Details** How is the electromagnetic spectrum divided?

_____

_____

_____

11. **Critical Thinking: Analyze** Explain the importance of wave-particle duality.

_____

_____

_____

12. **Inquiry Skill: Use Models** Draw a diagram that models the interactions of light with objects. Include reflection, refraction, and diffraction in your diagram.

13. **Test Prep** If light from a galaxy is shifted toward the blue end of the spectrum, what can you conclude about the galaxy's motion relative to Earth?

   A The galaxy is moving toward Earth.

   B The galaxy is moving slowly away from Earth.

   C The galaxy is moving rapidly away from Earth.

   D The motion of the galaxy relative to Earth is constantly changing.

© Houghton Mifflin Harcourt Publishing Company

What Is the Engineering Design Process?

Engineering

Engineering is the application of science, mathematics, and technology to design, test, and build machines, structures, processes, and systems that solve human problems. Engineers solve a variety of problems, from designing more fuel-efficient aircraft to developing earthquake-resistant building materials. There are many branches of engineering, including civil, mechanical, electrical, chemical, and aeronautical engineering. Engineers design and build bridges, cars, circuit boards, chemical compounds, and aircraft. Engineering is introduced to students in many education curriculums through STEM programs. STEM is an acronym for science, technology, engineering, and math.

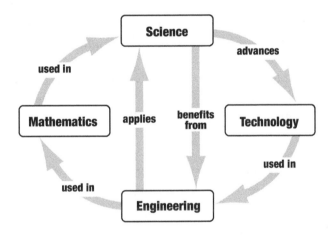

The Engineering Design Process

The engineering design process is the method that engineers use to solve a problem. The end result of the engineering design process is the development of a new machine, structure, process, or system.

The engineering design process begins with identifying a need. What is the problem that needs to be solved? Engineering problems are varied and can range from a need for better glass recycling technology to building a bridge to connect two points. Once the problem has been identified, research should be conducted into the problem. What is the status of other research into the problem? What are the constraints for solving the problem?

After the problem has been identified and researched, the next step is to brainstorm possible solutions. How could the problem be solved? Multiple solutions should be brainstormed to provide options for further evaluation. Promising solutions can be developed further, including adding drawings and illustrations of the solutions.

A solution based on all available information should be selected from all the ideas developed. Which idea best solves the problem? Which solution meets all of the constraints? Designing the actual solution should include building a model or prototype of the solution.

© Houghton Mifflin Harcourt Publishing Company

Once the model or prototype is built, the next step is to test and evaluate the solution. Were the results of the solution expected? The prototype should be evaluated against the problem to be solved and the constraints that were identified.

After evaluating the solution, improvements should be made. What changes could be made to provide better results? The solution can be redesigned, and the new model or prototype can be tested and evaluated. The process of redesign and evaluation is iterative, meaning it should be repeated until a satisfactory solution is achieved.

Defining and Delimiting a Problem

Possibly the most important step in the engineering design process is the definition of the problem to be solved and the development of design constraints. This is also known as defining and delimiting the problem. Having a clearly defined problem and a set of clearly delimited constraints will make the engineering design process easier, and solutions will be more applicable.

Problems with a narrower definition will be easier to solve than problems with a broader definition. For example, it will be easier to design a car engine that is 10% more fuel efficient than it will be to design a "better" car engine. The term "better" is too broad and will result in too many possible solutions that will be hard to narrow down.

Constraints are conditions that a design must meet. Constraints are used to refine and narrow the list of possible solutions to a problem. There are a wide variety of constraints that can be placed on an engineering problem. Sometimes constraints are mandatory, such as a size constraint. If you are designing a new car engine, there will be a mandatory constraint on how large the engine can be because it will have to fit in a designated space.

One of the greatest constraints can be safety. Engineers are responsible for designing and building bridges, buildings, and machines that the general public uses daily. This means engineers are responsible for the safety of many people.

Scientific principles can be used to specify constraints, and this is one of the many areas in which science and engineering overlap. As more constraints are added to a problem, the list of possible solutions becomes smaller and smaller. Eventually, there may only be a few, or possibly no, solutions which can meet all constraints and satisfactorily solve the problem.

© Houghton Mifflin Harcourt Publishing Company

What Is the Engineering Design Process?

Write the answers to the questions on the lines below.

1. What is engineering?

   _____

   _____

2. What are constraints?

   _____

3. What is the engineering design process?

   _____

4. What does STEM stand for?

   _____

5. Why are engineers often responsible for the safety of the general public?

   _____

   _____

6. What happens after a model or prototype is built during the engineering design process?

   _____

   _____

7. Name four branches of engineering.

   _____

8. **Vocabulary** Write a paragraph describing the engineering design process using the terms *engineer*, *problem*, and *constraint*.

   _____

   _____

   _____

   _____

© Houghton Mifflin Harcourt Publishing Company

9. **Main Idea** What are two factors that can make a problem easier to solve using the engineering design process?

_____

_____

_____

_____

10. **Reading Skill: Main Idea and Details** What is the end result of the engineering design process?

_____

_____

11. **Critical Thinking: Analyze** What is meant by the statement that the engineering design process is an iterative process?

_____

_____

_____

12. **Inquiry Skill: Infer** What could engineers do if no solution were found to a problem that met all design constraints?

_____

_____

_____

_____

13. **Test Prep** Which of the following is **NOT** a step in the engineering design process?

   A defining a problem

   B creating a problem

   C evaluating the solution

   D brainstorming solutions

© Houghton Mifflin Harcourt Publishing Company

How Are Engineering Design Solutions Evaluated?

The Engineering Design Process

The world is full of problems that can be solved. Humans have been using engineering techniques to solve problems for thousands of years. Even the use of simple levers and pulleys is considered to be an application of engineering principles.

The engineering design process is the method that engineers use to solve a problem. The end result of the engineering design process is the development of a new machine, structure, process, or system. The process consists of an iterative cycle that should produce an optimal solution.

The engineering design process begins with identifying and researching a problem. Possible solutions to the problem are brainstormed and promising ideas are developed further. Part of the brainstorming process is identifying the constraints that will be placed on the solution, such as size or cost. Eventually, a model or prototype of the solution is built to test against solving the problem and meeting the constraints. The prototype is evaluated, possible changes to the solution are brainstormed and discussed, and a new model is built and evaluated. The process continues until a satisfactory solution is found.

Evaluating the Solution

Solutions that are developed at the model or prototype stage must be tested and evaluated against the requirements of the solution. The requirements include two factors: adequately solving the intended problem and meeting all constraints. Some solutions may do a good job of solving the problem, but a poor job of meeting the design constraints. For example, a light car body made of carbon fiber may solve the problem of designing a more fuel-efficient car, but it might not meet cost constraints, since carbon fiber is relatively expensive when compared to plastic components.

Solutions should not be subjected to only one test. Solutions should be tested in a manner that allows engineers to identify potential weaknesses or strengths in the design. This means engineers must think creatively when deciding which tests the solution will be subjected to. Chemical engineers may do all of their testing and evaluating in a laboratory. Bioengineered solutions, such as genetically modified plants, may be tested and evaluated in the field.

125

The Evaluation Process

The process of testing, evaluating, and redesigning a solution should be a systematic process in which data are carefully collected, recorded, and analyzed. This will allow the engineering design team to select the best solution design from all of the designs tested. Data can be recorded in tables. Advantages and disadvantages of each solution can be added to the table to help engineers make their final decision.

Often, there is not one design that performs best over all the given tests. Sometimes, components of different designs that perform better on certain tests can be added together. This creates a new design that is a combination of previous designs and performs better overall on all tests.

Optimizing the Solution

The engineering design process is iterative so that engineers can develop an optimal solution. Each time the solution is tested, evaluated, and redesigned, it should meet the constraints and solve the problem more successfully.

Optimizing the solution can also include reevaluating the problem statement or reevaluating the design constraints. After one or two rounds of testing and evaluating solutions, it may become evident that the problem should be more clearly defined. Beginning with a problem that is as clearly defined as possible will make the process much easier.

Constraints can include factors such as a required size, a limited cost, or an expectation of product lifetime. As solutions are tested, evaluated, and redesigned, it may also become evident that there are either too many or too few restraints or that some restraints can be changed to provide more flexibility in the design. For example, an original list of constraints may have stated that a product of a certain size must last for 5 years and be produced for a certain cost. During the design process, it may be discovered that no material could be found that would make the product at the given size and cost that would last for 5 years. At this point, engineers would have to decide which constraint to change or relax. Would it be better to spend more money for a better material that will last for 5 years? Will the product really need to last for 5 years? If not, then one of the already existing solutions may solve the problem.

It is common to seek outside opinions during the evaluation phase of the process. Unbiased opinions can provide insights for team members and may also provide new ideas for how to positively change the design to better solve the problem and meet the constraints.

© Houghton Mifflin Harcourt Publishing Company

Name _____ Date _____

How Are Engineering Design Solutions Evaluated?

Fill in the blanks.

1. Engineers build a model or _____ to test against the problem constraints.

2. The _____ is the method used by engineers to solve a problem.

3. Maximum size or expected product lifetime are examples of _____ placed on the solution of a problem.

4. The use of simple _____ and _____ is considered to be an application of engineering principles.

5. The engineering process begins with _____ and _____ a problem.

6. The engineering design process is a(n) _____ process.

7. The world is full of _____ that can be solved.

8. **Main Idea** How do engineers optimize the design solution?

_____

_____

_____

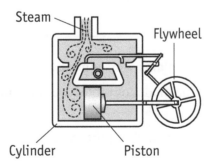

Steam

Flywheel

Cylinder

Piston

127

Engineering
Core Skills Science, Grade 7

9. **Vocabulary** Write a paragraph describing how engineering design solutions are evaluated. Use the terms *model*, *prototype*, *constraint*, and *process*.

_____

_____

_____

10. **Reading Skill: Main Ideas and Details** What are two examples of engineering solutions that humans have been using for thousands of years?

_____

_____

11. **Critical Thinking: Analyze** Why is it important that the testing and evaluation of design solutions be an orderly process?

_____

_____

_____

12. **Inquiry Skill: Infer** What might a group of engineers do if two of their designs were deemed to be optimal solutions?

_____

_____

_____

13. **Test Prep** Which of the following explains why engineering design solutions are evaluated?

   A Solutions that are developed to the model or prototype stage must be tested and evaluated to define the problem.

   B Solutions that are developed to the model or prototype stage must be tested and evaluated to define the constraints of the problem.

   C Solutions that are developed to the model or prototype stage must be tested and evaluated against the requirements of the solution.

   D Solutions that are developed to the model or prototype stage are not evaluated.

© Houghton Mifflin Harcourt Publishing Company

Answer Key

How Are Cell Structure and Function Related? LS1.A

1. e   2. a   3. d
4. g   5. b   6. c
7. f

8. Cells are made to perform certain functions. Single-celled organisms depend on specialized cell organelles to perform all of life's functions within the single cell. Multi-cellular organisms can have specialized cells that are meant to perform one or a handful of functions, such as red blood cells in humans delivering oxygen to the entire body.

9. The human body is made up of specialized cells that form tissues, organs, and then organ systems that are meant to perform specific functions.

10. Mitochondria are organelles that break down food to produce most of the ATP in a cell and in an organism.

11. Having the digestive enzymes enclosed inside lysosomes means they can perform their function of digesting food and breaking down wastes without affecting the contents of the entire cell.

12. Students should model a plant cell complete with organelles, including a cell wall, chloroplasts, and a large central vacuole.

13. B

How Do Plants Reproduce? LS1.B

1. f   2. d   3. a
4. e   5. g   6. c
7. b

8. Plants use asexual reproduction when they reproduce identical individuals, through nonspecialized structures such as tubers, plantlets, or runners. Plants use sexual reproduction during the alternation of generations life cycle. Male gametophytes are produced in the anthers and female gametophytes are produced in the ovaries. Sexual reproduction in plants involves the union of the gametes produced by the gametophytes.

9. Alternation of generations is a life cycle that alternates between a diploid sporophyte and a haploid gametophyte. The sporophyte produces haploid spores through meiosis. The gametophyte produces gametes by mitosis.

10. Pollination occurs when pollen is transferred from an anther to a stigma. The pollen grain travels down the style and fertilizes the embryo sac.

11. One advantage of asexual reproduction in plants is that it does not require pollination or another plant to reproduce. One disadvantage is that there is no opportunity for genetic diversity. All offspring are genetically identical to the parent plant.

12. Pollinators are important to plants because they help plants transfer pollen from anthers to stigmas. Plants cannot move, so without animals spreading pollen while visiting flowers, plants would have to rely solely on the wind for pollination. Without pollination in flowering plants, there would be no fertilization and no reproduction. This means pollinators are also important for humans and the flowering crops that we rely on for food.

13. B

How Does Photosynthesis Cycle Matter and Energy? LS1.C

1. photosynthesis
2. chloroplasts
3. pigment
4. electron transport chain
5. reactants
6. matter, energy
7. Plants are some of the organisms that conduct photosynthesis. During photosynthesis, the pigment chlorophyll in the chloroplasts of plants capture energy from sunlight to form sugar and oxygen from carbon dioxide and water.

8. The substances that are need for photosynthesis, or the reactants, are carbon dioxide and water. The substances that are produced by photosynthesis, or the products, are sugars and oxygen.

9. Since animals do not have chloroplasts, this means they cannot produce their own food, and so they must be consumers. This means animals must consume, or eat, other organisms to acquire energy their cells can use.

10. The content of the bubble of gas must be oxygen because that is the gas produced by photosynthesis, and the plant must have been conducting photosynthesis while it was kept in sunlight.

11. B

How Do Humans Respond to Stimuli? LS1.D

1. Homeostasis
2. stimulus
3. negative feedback
4. photoreceptors
5. nervous system
6. axon
7. Shivering
8. Humans respond to stimuli by gathering the information with sensory organs, passing the information to the brain, processing the information in the brain, and responding to the information through a physical action or by forming a memory.

9. The human body uses sensory organs and nerve cells to gather information from the environment. The information from the environment is in the

129

form of stimuli that cause a response. Nerve cells pass nerve signals to the brain, where the information is processed. The brain can send signals to cause a physical response, or the brain can store the information as a memory.

10. Nerve cells in the eyes are photoreceptors that can detect light. Nerve cells in the ears can detect sound waves.

11. Accurate and rapid information processing by the brain is important to maintain homeostasis and prevent major damage to the human body. It is also important during stressful or dangerous moments.

12. My body responds to the stimulus of a favorite smell by thinking of positive memories. My body responds to a dark room by dilating my pupils and moving slowly to prevent injury.

13. B

What Are Food Webs? LS2.B

1. A scavenger is an animal that feeds on dead animals and plants.

2. A decomposer is an organism that gets energy by breaking down, or decomposing, dead organisms.

3. A producer is an organism that changes the energy in sunlight into chemical energy, or energy in food.

4. A consumer is an organism that must consume other organisms to obtain energy.

5. An arrow in a food web shows the direction energy is transferred.

6. Food chains and food webs are alike because they both show how energy is transferred within a living system. Food chains and food webs are different because food chains only show one source of food for each consumer and food webs try to

model many, or all, sources of food for consumers in a system.

7. Omnivores are consumers that eat plants and animals. Carnivores are consumers that eat only animals. Herbivores are consumers that eat only plants.

8. Decomposers are known as "nature's recyclers" because they break down and return valuable nutrients to soil and water.

9. Scavengers and decomposers are also considered consumers because they get their energy from other organisms, not from the sun like a producer.

10. Students should draw a logical food web that includes producers, decomposers, and consumers.

11. D

What Is Meiosis? LS3.A

1. chromosomes   2. cytokinesis
3. sexual   4. homologous
5. haploid   6. crossing-over
7. Gametes

8. A mitotic cell division results in two identical cells, each with a full set of chromosomes. A meiotic cell division results in four haploid cells, each with half a set of chromosomes.

9. Meiosis results in four haploid gametes, which can then be used in sexual reproduction. The union of two haploid gametes results in a diploid organism.

10. Genetic diversity can be increased during meiosis when genes cross over and when chromosomes are sorted independently.

11. If sex cells had a full set of chromosomes, then the union of two sex cells would result in an individual with two times the correct number of chromosomes.

12. Students should create a graphic organizer that models meiosis.

13. D

How Are Fossils Evidence of Common Ancestry? LS4.A

1. record
2. 4.6 billion
3. homologous
4. fossil
5. Charles Darwin
6. mineralization
7. tree of life

8. Fossil evidence of similar anatomical or developmental structures, embryological development, and similarities in biological molecules can all be used to infer common ancestry between organisms, either living or represented in the fossil record.

9. Fossils can form when organisms are buried in sedimentary rock, trapped and preserved in resin, trapped and preserved in asphalt, frozen and preserved in cold climates, or petrified through mineralization. All of the fossils on Earth make up the fossil record.

10. Fossils are rare because specific conditions must exist for a fossil to form. These conditions are not always present to fossilize or preserve an organism, so many organisms that form Earth's history may be undocumented in the fossil record.

11. The rarity of fossils impacts the fossil record because the fossil record cannot be depended upon to provide a complete picture of the history of life on Earth. Many organisms from Earth's history may be undocumented in the fossil record because they lived and died in conditions that were not conducive to preservation and fossilization.

12. I would compare the anatomical structures of the organism to existing species. For example, if the organism had a backbone, then I would infer that it is part of the evolutionary line of descent

© Houghton Mifflin Harcourt Publishing Company

Answer Key
Core Skills Science, Grade 7

the evolutionary line of descent of vertebrates.

13. C

What Is Artificial Selection?
LS4.B

1. monohybrid
2. selective breeding
3. Evolution
4. Farmers, breeders
5. genotype
6. genetic
7. alleles
8. Artificial selection works in the same manner as natural selection, only humans, not nature, are applying the selective pressure. This means that humans are preferentially selecting organisms to breed based on desired characteristics.
9. Artificial selection is similar to natural selection, only humans are proving the filter for choosing which organisms reproduce instead of nature or the organism's environment. Today, modern genetics are used to fully understand and harness the technique of artificial selection.
10. The set of alleles that an individual has for a characteristic is called the genotype. The trait that results from a set of alleles is the phenotype. In other words, genotype determines phenotype. Phenotype can also be affected by conditions in the environment, such as nutrients and temperature.
11. Genetic variation is a key component of natural selection and artificial selection because without variation, there wouldn't be anything for nature or humans to select for.
12. First, scientists would need to determine which plants in a population are resistant to the pest. Then, scientists could breed only those plants. The resulting generation could again

be evaluated for resistance to the pest, and resistant plant from the first generation could be bred. This process could continue until a new plant that is resistant to the pest is developed.

13. C

How Do Adaptations Help Organisms Survive? LS4.C

1. A fixed action pattern behavior is a type of innate behavior that always occurs the same way, such as orb spiders always building the same web.
2. Natural selection is the process by which organisms that are better adapted to their environment survive and reproduce more successfully than less well-adapted organisms.
3. Adaptations are important because they can help organisms survive and reproduce, and adaptations also provide variable traits for natural selection.
4. The process in which populations gradually change over time is called evolution.
5. Fishes use their gills to breathe. Oxygen in the water passes through the thin membrane of the gills to the blood. The blood then carries oxygen through the body. Gills are also used to remove carbon dioxide from the blood.
6. Instincts are innate behaviors that are genetically inherited.
7. Adaptations make organisms more capable of surviving and reproducing in their environment.
8. Evolution is the gradual genetic change of populations over time. Natural selection is the mechanism by which evolution works and natural selection acts by choosing organisms better adapted to their environments.
9. Adaptations are characteristics

that help an organism increase their chance of survival and reproduction. Adaptations are dependent on an organism's environment, as traits that may be favorable in one habitat may be unfavorable in other habitats. Adaptations can be physical characteristics or behaviors.

10. Fishes have strong muscles, fins, scales, and gills, which are all adaptations that help them swim.
11. Innate behaviors, or instincts, are inherited and can be considered to be adaptations if they help an organism survive and reproduce in its environment.
12. A favorable trait in a desert environment could be a plant's deep root system that allows it to reach more ground water. An unfavorable trait in a desert environment could be an animal with thick fur. The plant's deep root system would be considered an adaptation because it would help the plant survive and reproduce.

13. A

What Is Biodiversity? LS4.D

1. Extinction occurs when a species no longer exists on Earth.
2. The Endangered Species Act is a federal law that protects species on the endangered list and prohibits activities that could harm the species.
3. Banana plants are genetically very similar to each other. This makes them susceptible to disease. Banana farmers have found that increasing the biodiversity of banana fields by growing other plants among the bananas can lead to healthier banana plants.
4. Biodiversity increases productivity, prevents specific diseases from wiping out entire ecosystems, and provides a variety of organisms to fill

131

niche roles in the ecosystem.

5. Increased species richness leads to increased productivity in an ecosystem.

6. Endangered species can be protected by preserving their habitats.

7. Biodiversity is the variety of organisms, their genetic differences, and the communities and ecosystems in which they occur. Biodiversity includes both species richness, which is a measure of the number of different species in a community, and species diversity, which is the relative numbers of each of the species present in a community.

8. Some see the rain forests as a resource to be developed, either for the timber or to create farm land. This is how the North American forests were viewed over a century ago.

9. An extinct species' prey would possibly undergo a population increase because of the decrease in predation. This could lead to a dwindling food supply for the prey, as well as other organisms, which could eventually lead to mass starvation. The extinct species' predator may undergo a population decrease as one of its food sources is no longer available.

10. Students should list all of the plants, animals, and microorganisms within their chosen ecosystem. Students should also make a note of species richness and species diversity.

11. D

What Is the Universe? ESS1.A
1. Milky Way   2. Big Bang
3. galaxy   4. universe
5. binary   6. Doppler
7. galactic group
8. Most scientists accept the Big Bang theory as a valid explanation for the formation of

the universe. The Big Bang theory suggests that all matter and energy was once compressed into a very small volume. All of this matter and energy exploded in every direction, forming the expanding universe.

9. The universe consists of all the matter and energy that exists. Planets are part of solar systems, which are part of galaxies. All of these components are part of the universe.

10. The sun is different from most other stars because it is not part of binary system or multiple-star system.

11. The Doppler effect is a perceived shift in the wavelength of a galaxy due to its movement towards or away from Earth. Scientists have discovered that the wavelengths of most galaxies are red shifted, meaning that the galaxies are moving away from Earth. This is evidence that the universe is expanding away from Earth in all directions.

12. A binary system consists of two stars orbiting each other. A star cluster consists of a group of stars that travel through space together bound by gravity.

13. C

What Makes Up the Solar System? ESS1.B
1. The nebular hypothesis is the hypothesis formed by Laplace in 1796 that explains the formation of the solar system.

2. The best place to find asteroids in the solar system would be the asteroid belt between Mars and Jupiter.

3. A dwarf planet is different from a planet because a dwarf planet has not cleared its orbit of debris.

4. A comet is a body of ice, rock, and gases that orbits the sun.

5. During the formation of the solar system, the majority of the matter ended up in the sun.

6. Pluto and Ceres are dwarf planets.

7. A solar system includes a star and the objects that orbit it.

8. Moons are natural satellites that orbit a planet.

9. A solar system is a star and all of the objects that orbit the star. Parts of a solar system can include gas giant and terrestrial planets, moons, asteroids, comets, and dwarf planets.

10. Planets formed in the solar nebula as matter condensed due to gravity and collided to form ever larger bodies orbiting the sun. Planetesimals joined together to form protoplanets, which attracted other planetesimals through the force of gravity. Eventually, the protoplanets became very large and dense and they formed the planets and the moons.

11. The planet order from closest to the sun to farthest from the sun is Mercury, Venus, Earth, Mars, Jupiter, Saturn, Uranus, and Neptune.

12. Gravity is important in a solar system because it keeps objects orbiting the central star, as well as orbiting other smaller objects, such as a moon orbiting a planet. Gravity is also critical to the development of a solar system from a solar nebula.

13. Students should draw a solar system with a star at the center and other objects orbiting the star.

14. B

What Is the Geologic Time Scale? ESS1.C
1. Geology   2. explosion
3. Phanerozoic   4. Paleocene
5. fossil record 6. Holocene
7. Mesozoic
8. The geologic time scale is a way to divide the history of life

© Houghton Mifflin Harcourt Publishing Company

on Earth based on large events such as mass extinctions or the flourishing of a particular group of organisms.

9. The geologic time scale is divided into increasingly smaller divisions. The largest time divisions are eons, followed by eras, periods, epochs, and ages.

10. Both the Permian period and the Cretaceous period ended in mass extinctions and marked the end of their respective eras.

11. The geologic time scale covers a very large time span. It is easier for scientists to mark the time by major historical events instead of by set time increments because changes of similar magnitude occurred irregularly throughout Earth's history.

12. Students should draw a geologic time scale that includes eons, eras, periods, and epochs.

13. A

How Does Earth Change?
ESS2.A

1. Earth's hot interior is the source of energy for tectonic processes.

2. The solid part of Earth that consists of all rock, as well as the soils and loose rocks on Earth's surface, makes up the geosphere.

3. Earth is approximately 4.6 billion years old.

4. Digging into the ground is digging into the lithosphere.

5. Scientists have concluded that the outer core of Earth is liquid.

6. Earth's structural layers from deepest to shallowest are the inner core, the outer core, the mesosphere, the asthenosphere, and the lithosphere.

7. Matter is anything that has mass and takes up space. Energy is the ability to do work.

8. Erosion is the removal of weathered sediments.

9. Matter and energy constantly

cycle in and between the smaller systems that make up the larger Earth system. If a large amount of energy is transferred, as in a volcanic eruption, then Earth's crust can shake, move, and be rearranged. If a large amount of mass is involved in a process, such as the convection of rock in the mantle, then Earth's crust may also move, like the movement of tectonic plates.

10. Earth can be divided into layers based on the chemical composition of the rock or the structure of the rock. The compositional layers are the crust, the mantle, and the core. The crust is the outermost layer and the core is the innermost layer. The structural layers are the lithosphere, the asthenosphere, the mesosphere, the outer core, and the inner core.

11. Scientists make conclusions about the composition and depth of Earth's layers by studying seismic waves as they move through the geosphere.

12. Earth's crust can change through processes such as erosion and tectonic processes. Erosion, the removal of weathered sediments, can occur very slowly, such as when a river erodes a deep canyon. Erosion can also happen very quickly, like during a flash flood or a landslide. Tectonic processes are driven by the movement of tectonic plates. Changes to Earth's crust through the movement of tectonic plates can happen very slowly since the plates only travel a few centimeters each year. Changes due to tectonic processes can also happen very quickly, like the release of energy during an earthquake.

13. Students should draw a diagram of the structural and

compositional layers of Earth. A drawing to scale will show the crust as the thinnest layer by far. Convection occurs within the mantle, which is made up of the asthenosphere and the mesosphere.

14. C

What Is the Rock Cycle?
ESS2.A

1. Limestone is formed by calcite.

2. Granite is made of quartz and feldspar, and granite forms when liquid rock cools and solidifies.

3. High temperature and pressure are required to transform sedimentary rock into metamorphic rock.

4. Limestone is a sedimentary rock made of calcite that forms when sediments are buried and put under pressure.

5. Geologists classify rocks into three major classes based on how they are formed.

6. Marble is a metamorphic rock that forms when rock is placed under intense heat and pressure.

7. The rock cycle describes how rocks constantly change from one form to another.

8. Igneous rock, metamorphic rock, and sedimentary rock are the three types of rock involved in the rock cycle.

9. A sedimentary rock can become a metamorphic rock when it is subjected to intense temperatures and pressure. A metamorphic rock can become an igneous rock when the rock is melted and then cooled. An igneous rock can become a sedimentary rock when it is weathered into sediments, eroded, and the sediments are compressed and cemented together.

10. Metamorphic rock is formed when intense heat and pressure change the structure, texture, or composition of sedimentary rock.

© Houghton Mifflin Harcourt Publishing Company

11. The rock cycle involves the transformation of one type of rock into a different type. When a new rock is formed, it comes from an existing rock. Matter is neither created nor destroyed. Instead, it is conserved as the rock transforms.

12. Basalt is an igneous rock. Basalt can become a sedimentary rock when it is weathered into sediments, eroded, and the sediments are compressed and cemented together.

13. C

How Does Water Cycle on Earth? ESS2.C

1. b	**2.** g	**3.** e
4. f	**5.** c	**6.** a
7. d		

8. Evaporation takes place mainly over the oceans. This is because the oceans are vast and most of the water on Earth is in the oceans. Energy from the sun causes evaporation from the oceans.

9. The water cycle is the movement of water between the oceans, the atmosphere, living things, and Earth's surface. During evaporation, liquid water changes to water vapor when energy is added to a system. Transpiration is the evaporation of water from the leaves of a plant. During condensation, water vapor cools and changes back to liquid droplets. During precipitation, water droplets fall to Earth's surface.

10. Clouds form in the atmosphere through the process of condensation. Millions of tiny water droplets come together to form clouds.

11. The sun's role in the water cycle is to provide the energy necessary for evaporation to occur.

12. Students should model the path of a water droplet through the water cycle. They should include the processes of evaporation, condensation, and precipitation.

13. A

What Is Weather? ESS2.D

1. A daily forecast is most accurate because it only forecasts up to 48 hours in advance.

2. Hurricanes build strength over warm, tropical ocean waters.

3. Cold fronts can bring thunderstorms, heavy rain, or snow.

4. A system must have wind speeds of at least 120 km/h to be classified as a hurricane.

5. The condensation of water vapor within large storms releases a large amount of energy that fuels the storms.

6. Meteorology is the study of the atmosphere.

7. A typhoon is a hurricane in the western Pacific Ocean.

8. Hurricanes lose strength when they make landfall because they are no longer over the warm waters that provide large amounts of energy for the storm through evaporation and condensation.

9. Weather is the condition of the atmosphere at a specific location and time. Weather can include aspects such as how hot or cold it is or how stormy, rainy, or clear it is at a given location.

10. The four main types of weather fronts are cold fronts, warm fronts, occluded fronts, and stationary fronts. A cold front occurs when cold air moves under less dense warm air, pushing the warm air up. A warm front occurs when warm air moves over colder, denser air. An occluded front forms when a warm air mass is caught between two colder air masses. A stationary front forms when a cold air mass meets a warm air mass. In this case, however, neither air mass has enough force to move the other.

11. Nowcasts mainly use radar and enable forecasters to focus on timing precipitation and tracking severe weather. Daily forecasts predict weather conditions for a 48-hour period. Extended forecasts look ahead 3 to 7 days. Medium-range forecasts look ahead 8 to 14 days. Long-range forecasts cover monthly and seasonal periods.

12. Oceans absorb, store, and globally redistribute energy from the sun. This energy is a critical input for many weather systems, so oceans play a large role in Earth's weather.

13. Students should create a graphic organizer that shows the steps in developing a weather forecast. Steps should include collecting data, interpreting data, and making predictions. Students can also include tools used, and the different types of forecasts that can be developed.

14. A

What Are Minerals? ESS3.A

1. The mineralogist can learn the density of the mineral.

2. Cleavage is the tendency of a mineral to break, creating a new smooth edge.

3. To identify a mineral by using the Mohs hardness scale, I'd try to scratch the surface of a mineral with the edge of one of the reference minerals. If the reference mineral scratched my mineral, the reference mineral would be harder than my mineral.

4. The way a surface reflects light is called luster.

5. A mineral's streak can be found by rubbing the mineral against a piece of unglazed porcelain called a streak plate. The mark left on the streak plate is the streak.

6. Impurities and other factors can change the appearance of minerals. This makes color an

© Houghton Mifflin Harcourt Publishing Company

unreliable characteristic for identifying minerals.

7. The ratio of an object's density to the density of water is called the object's specific gravity.

8. A mineral is a natural, usually inorganic solid that has a characteristic chemical composition, an orderly internal structure, and a characteristic set of physical properties, such as density, streak, hardness, luster, cleavage, and color. Rocks are the material that make up the solid part of Earth's crust. Rocks can be composed of one or more minerals, or may not be composed of minerals at all.

9. The physical properties of minerals include color, density, streak, luster, cleavage, fracture, and hardness. Streak describes the color of a mineral in powder form. Luster describes how a mineral reflects light. Cleavage and fracture describe how a mineral breaks. Hardness describes a mineral's resistance to being scratched. Minerals have characteristic densities that can be used to identify them.

10. Minerals are a nonrenewable natural resource that come from the environment. Mineral resources can be either metals, such as gold, silver, and aluminum, or nonmetals, such as sulfur and quartz. Some metals are prized for their beauty and rarity. Certain rare nonmetallic minerals called gemstones display extraordinary brilliance and color when they are specifically cut for jewelry. Other nonmetallic minerals, such as calcite and gypsum, are used as building materials. Table salt is derived from the nonmetallic mineral halite.

11. There are two minerals on the Mohs hardness scale that could scratch feldspar, but could not scratch corundum. Quartz and topaz share this property because they are harder than feldspar, but softer than corundum.

12. Most minerals are nonrenewable resources because they take a long time to form. Minerals are also distributed unevenly around the globe due to differences in Earth processes, as well as different distribution of elements around the globe. Minerals such as rare metals and gemstones can be very valuable. Local economies where these minerals are mined may be strong due to the global demand for these minerals.

13. B

What Are Natural Hazards?
ESS3.B

1. e	2. g	3. a
4. b	5. h	6. d
7. f	8. c	

9. Scientists study natural hazards in an effort to understand them more. If scientists understand why, how, and where natural hazards occur, they may be able to forecast the hazards with more accuracy, which could preserve human property and lives.

10. Natural hazards are naturally occurring phenomena that can damage natural habitats and human property. An earthquake is a sudden movement of Earth's crust that releases energy. The release of energy can damage habitats and buildings and even kill people. A volcano is a mountain that can erupt violently. A tornado is a storm with rotating winds that can cause extreme damage. Mass movement is the movement of fragments down a slope. Mass movement can be very destructive. Different types of mass movement can be caused by different types of natural hazards.

11. Mass movement on a slope can be prevented by replanting the slope if it is bare, or by constructing terraces or retaining walls.

12. A mudflow is caused by heavy rainfall or a volcanic eruption in a dry, mountainous area. The rapid addition of moisture to dry soil on a steep slope can start a flow of mud downslope. Large mudflows can be very destructive as they move downslope, destroying anything that gets in their way, including natural habitats and human property.

13. The unpredictability of natural hazards makes them dangerous because it makes it hard for people to be in a safe location at the right time.

14. C

How Do Humans Impact Earth? ESS3.C

1. An exotic species is one that is not native to a region.

2. A nonrenewable resource is one that cannot be replaced or that can be replaced only over thousands or millions of years.

3. Pollution is an unwanted change in the environment caused by substances such as wastes or by forms of energy such as radiation.

4. Exotic species are not native to a region. Invasive species are exotic species that have had extreme success in their new environments.

5. Air pollutants include the compounds carbon monoxide, nitrogen oxide, sulfur dioxide, and volatile organic compounds. Most of these pollutants can come from burning fossil fuels.

6. Burmese pythons are an invasive species in Florida. They prey on the endangered Key Largo wood rat.

7. Habitat fragmentation occurs when human activity makes part of an ecosystem inaccessible.

8. As the human population increases, there is a need for

© Houghton Mifflin Harcourt Publishing Company

need, humans have to develop additional quantities of known resources, such as logging additional forests or drilling more wells for oil. As the number of people increases so does the human impact on Earth.

9. Earth has many natural resources, such as water, fossil fuels, minerals, and biodiversity. A renewable resource is one that can be replaced at the same rate that the resource is used. Solar and wind energy are renewable resources. A nonrenewable resource is one that cannot be replaced or that can be replaced only over thousands or millions of years. Most minerals and fossil fuels are nonrenewable resources.

10. Burning fossil fuels can cause pollution, such as the formation of acid rain.

11. At first, noxious weeds may increase the biodiversity of an ecosystem slightly because there would be an additional species and an increased number of organisms within the ecosystem. However, as the noxious weeds began to out-compete local plants, the biodiversity of the ecosystem could decrease dramatically as local plants are removed from the ecosystem.

12. If we do not find better ways to minimize human impact, the Earth system will continue to be polluted by fossil fuel emissions and chemicals, depleted of its resources, overrun by exotic species, and destroyed and fragmented by habitat destruction.

13. A

What Is Climate Change?
ESS3.D

1. Weather is short-term atmospheric events that happen on a relatively local scale.

2. On average, Earth's climate is currently getting warmer, which leads to a variety of changes to global and local weather patterns.

3. Volcanic eruptions can naturally cause climate change by releasing gases and particulates into the atmosphere.

4. This energy is distributed unevenly around the globe through convection currents in the atmosphere and in the oceans.

5. A carbon sink is anything in the environment that absorbs and stores carbon.

6. Scientists think the burning of fossil fuels in power plants, factories, and automobile engines is the cause of rising global carbon emissions.

7. Currently, human activities release about 21 billion tons of carbon dioxide into the air each year.

8. Climate change refers to long-term, significant changes to temperatures and weather patterns on a global scale.

9. Climate is the average weather conditions of an area over a given period of time. Lasting and substantial changes to the climate are known as climate change. Climate change that is marked by an increase in global temperatures is known as global warming.

10. Sunspots are regions of the sun that are cooler than the surrounding areas. Sunspot activity on the sun goes through an eleven-year cycle. Periods of higher sunspot activity are associated with warming trends on Earth, which can affect the global climate. Periods of decreased sunspot activity are associated with cooling trends on Earth, which can also affect the global climate.

11. Scientific predictions concerning climate change are important to human society because society needs to understand the factors that contribute to climate change, the risks of global climate change, and steps we can take to prevent or reverse climate change.

12. Scientists predict that by 2035, the amount of carbon emissions will be equal between developing and developed countries. This will mark a decrease in emissions for developed countries and an increase in emissions for developing countries.

13. A

What Is the Periodic Table?
PS1.A

1. metals
2. atomic number
3. seven
4. protons
5. nonmetals
6. chemical symbol
7. family
8. Elements on the periodic table are arranged by increasing atomic number. They are also arranged into horizontal rows, called periods, and vertical columns, called groups.
9. Metals are elements to the left of the zigzag line. Metals are shiny and conduct heat and electricity. Nonmetals are elements to the right of the zigzag line. Nonmetals are dull and brittle. Metalloids are elements bordering the zigzag line. Metalloids share the properties of metals and nonmetals.
10. A vertical column of elements on the periodic table is known as a group. Elements in the same group tend to have similar chemical and physical properties because they have similar electron arrangements and reactivity. A horizontal row of elements on the periodic table is known as a period. The physical and chemical properties of

136

and chemical properties of elements in a period change in a predictable way across the periodic table.

11. The zigzag line separates metals, nonmetals, and metalloids on the periodic table. Without any other information about an element, knowing where it is placed in relation to the zigzag line can give information about how well the element conducts electricity or heat, or if the element is malleable.

12. Elements in the same group have similar properties because they have the same number of electrons in their outer energy level. If you know what group an element belongs to, you can predict the properties of that element based on the properties of other elements in the same group.

13. D

How Is Mass Conserved in Chemical Reactions? PS1.B

1. equation
2. created, destroyed
3. Reactants
4. mole
5. mass, energy
6. Antoine Lavoisier
7. chemical reaction
8. A chemical reaction involves reactants coming together to form new products. The total mass of reactants in a chemical reaction equals the total mass of the products due to the conservation of mass.
9. The Law of Conservation of Mass states that matter cannot be created or destroyed in an ordinary chemical reaction.
10. An exothermic reaction releases energy to the surroundings as heat. An endothermic reaction absorbs energy from the surroundings to break the bonds of the reactants.
11. Since mass is conserved, and the number of atoms of each element

must be the same in the products and the reactants, you can infer that there are three atoms of oxygen in the reactants.

12. This does not violate the Law of Conservation of Mass because the ashes are not the only product of the chemical reaction. Some of the matter in the log was converted to compounds that are gases that entered the atmosphere.

13. C

What Is Nuclear Fusion? PS1.C
(HIGH SCHOOL)

1. fusion
2. fission
3. hydrogen
4. mass
5. chain
6. core
7. Earth depends on energy, such as light and heat, from the sun. This energy is produced through nuclear fusion. Without light and heat, life on Earth would not exist.
8. Nuclear fusion that takes place in the sun is known as solar fusion. Nuclear fusion occurs in the sun when hydrogen nuclei are combined to form helium atoms.
9. During nuclear fusion, lighter nuclei are combined to form heavier elements. During nuclear fission, heavier elements are split to form nuclei of lighter elements. Both reactions produce large amounts of energy.
10. Fusion requires very high temperatures of at least 15,000,000°C. We don't fuse hydrogen on Earth because it is too difficult to create the conditions necessary for fusion.
11. Students should diagram nuclear fusion. Diagrams should include multiple hydrogen nuclei coming together to from a helium nucleus by emitting a positron and combining two protons with a neutron.
12. A

What Are Newton's Laws of Motion? PS2.A

1. reaction
2. mass
3. acceleration
4. third
5. Sir Isaac Newton
6. unbalanced
7. force
8. Newton's laws of motion explain the interaction of forces and objects. The first law states that an object at rest will stay at rest, and an object in motion will stay in motion, unless acted on by an unbalanced force. The second law describes the motion of an object when an unbalanced force acts on the object. The third law states that all forces act in pairs.
9. A force is a push or pull that is exerted on an object. Net force is calculated by adding up all the forces that are acting on an object. When the net force is zero, the forces are balanced. Balanced forces will not cause a change in acceleration. When the net force is not zero, the forces are unbalanced. Unbalanced forces cause an object to change speed or direction of motion, or both.
10. Unbalanced forces cause a change in speed or direction of motion, or both.
11. Newton's second law of motion states that force is equal to mass times acceleration. Using this relationship, there are two ways to increase the acceleration of an object. The force applied to the object can be increased, or the mass of the object can be decreased. Both of these situations would lead to an increase in acceleration.
12. Student should draw a diagram that shows the foot exerting a force on the ball and the ball exerting a force on the foot that is equal in magnitude, but opposite in direction. The action and reaction forces do not cancel

© Houghton Mifflin Harcourt Publishing Company

each other out because they are acting on two different objects. This is how motion occurs.

13. D

What Are Electromagnetic Forces? PS2.B

1. The strong nuclear force keeps the protons in a nucleus from flying away from one another.
2. Gravity is the weakest of the four fundamental forces.
3. The process by which an electric current is made by changing a magnetic field is called electromagnetic induction.
4. The electric force is a universal force that exists between any two charged objects.
5. An electromagnet is made up of a solenoid wrapped around an iron core.
6. The electric force between two charged objects depends upon the amount of charge on each object and the distance between them.
7. A solenoid is a coil of wire that produces a magnetic field when carrying an electric current.
8. Electromagnetic forces are related forces that arise from the interaction of electric and magnetic fields.
9. A force is a push or a pull on an object. Electromagnetic forces arise from the interaction between magnetic and electrical fields. A solenoid is a coil of wire that produces a magnetic field when it is carrying an electric current. An electromagnet is a solenoid wrapped around an iron core. Both solenoids and electromagnets are examples of the interaction of electromagnetic forces.
10. An electric generator in a power plant uses electromagnetic induction to change mechanical energy into electrical energy.
11. An electromagnet becomes stronger as the current increases,

so an electric current of 1000 amperes would produce a stronger electromagnet.
12. An electromagnet becomes just a magnet if the electric current is shut off. This greatly reduces the strength of the magnetic field.
13. B
14. A

What Is Kinetic Energy? PS3.A

1. a	2. e	3. g
4. d	5. f	6. h
7. c	8. b	

9. Energy is the ability to do work. Work is done when a force causes an object to move in the direction of the force. When one object does work on another, energy is transferred from the first object to the second object. There are many types of energy. Energy can be converted from one form to another or transferred from object to another, but it is never created or destroyed. This is the Law of Conservation of Energy.
10. The energy an object has due to its motion is called kinetic energy. The magnitude of kinetic energy is dependent upon mass and speed. The energy an object has due to its position is space is called potential energy. Mechanical energy is the total energy of motion and position of an object. Mechanical energy can be all kinetic energy, all potential energy, or both kinetic and potential energy.
11. Kinetic energy depends on the speed and the mass of an object.
12. The apples are suspended above the ground on limbs of the apple tree. The apples have potential energy because they have stored energy due to their position above the ground.
13. Students should draw an object that is moving on the ground without potential energy, an object that has energy of position, but not energy of

motion, and an object that is both moving and also has energy of position, such as an airplane flying through the air.

14. B

What Is Conservation of Energy? PS3.A

1. matter, energy
2. Energy, matter, momentum
3. conversion
4. open
5. theory
6. created, destroyed
7. isolated
8. The Law of Conservation of Energy states that energy cannot be created or destroyed during ordinary chemical and physical changes.
9. A system in which energy and matter are exchanged with the surroundings is an open system. If energy but not matter is exchanged, the system is closed. An isolated system is one in which neither energy nor matter is exchanged.
10. When I watch TV after school, the electrical energy is converted to light energy and sound energy. When I ride my bike, the mechanical energy of pedaling is converted to kinetic energy of the bike moving forward. When I use a flashlight, the chemical energy in the batteries is converted to light energy. In all of these systems, the total energy remains the same even though the energy is converted from one type to another.
11. Nuclear reactions on the sun can cause the conversion between mass and energy. The total amount of mass and equivalent energy is still conserved, however, even though one is converted into the other. The Earth receives energy from the sun that is reradiated to space. So the Earth-sun is not an isolated system. In general, energy on Earth cannot be created or

© Houghton Mifflin Harcourt Publishing Company

destroyed since almost all reactions are normal chemical or physical changes.

12. It is important to know whether a system is open, closed, or isolated because a scientist must account for all areas where matter or energy can be transferred or lost from a system. This will help scientists interpret the results of their experiments and design better experiments.

13. C

What Are Sound Waves? PS4.A

1. A   2. C   3. C
4. longitudinal, transverse
5. resonance
6. Mechanical
7. frequency
8. Sound waves are a type of mechanical wave. Sound waves have all of the characteristics of mechanical waves, such as frequency, wavelength, amplitude, and speed. Sound waves also require a material medium to transfer energy.

9. All waves can be characterized by the same properties, including wavelength, frequency, amplitude, and speed. The wavelength of a wave is the distance between any point on a wave and the corresponding point on the next wave. The number of waves produced in a given amount of time is the frequency of the wave. The amplitude of a wave is related to its height and the speed of a wave is equal to the wave frequency multiplied by the wavelength.

10. Mechanical waves require a medium to transfer energy. Electromagnetic waves can travel through a medium, but electromagnetic waves can also travel through a vacuum.

11. The amplitude of a wave is related to its height. For a mechanical wave, the amplitude is the maximum distance that the

particles of a medium vibrate from their rest position. It makes sense that a wave with a larger amplitude would carry more energy than a wave with a smaller amplitude because it would take more energy to move the particles farther from their rest position.

12. 8.2 cm
13. A

How Does Light Interact with Objects? PS4.B

1. Light waves have been reflected if they bounce off an object.

2. If light travels from one transparent medium air to another water at any angle other than straight on, the light ray changes direction when it meets the boundary.

3. EM waves are different from other waves because they do not need a medium to travel through.

4. Light waves transmit energy.

5. The relative motion between a wave source and an observer creates an apparent frequency shift known as the Doppler effect.

6. electric field and magnetic field

7. Interference occurs when waves of similar wavelength occur in the same area. They can combine to produce a single new wave that is different from the original waves.

8. Waves that can transfer energy without going through a medium are electromagnetic waves. Visible light is one example. The entire range of EM waves is called the electromagnetic spectrum.

9. Visible light interacts with objects through reflection, refraction, and diffraction. Reflection occurs when light encounters an object that is opaque to part of the light. Part of the light is absorbed and the rest of it is reflected at the surface. Refraction occurs when

light passes from one medium to another at an angle. Diffraction occurs when light waves pass the edge of an object.

10. The EM spectrum is divided into regions according to the length of the waves. The greater the frequency of an electromagnetic wave, the more energy it transmits.

11. Wave-particle duality is important because there are some behaviors of light that are explained by a wave model and some behaviors of light that are explained by a particle model. Wave-particle duality allows scientists to form a comprehensive view of the behavior of light.

12. Students should draw a diagram that correctly shows light interacting with objects through reflection, refraction, and diffraction.

13. A

What Is the Engineering Design Process? ETS1.A

1. Engineering is the application of science, mathematics, and technology to design, test, and build machines, structures, processes, and systems that solve human problems.

2. Constraints are conditions that a design must meet.

3. The engineering design process is the method that engineers use to solve a problem.

4. STEM stands for science, technology, engineering, and mathematics.

5. Engineers are often responsible for the safety of the general public because they build structures and machines that the public uses daily.

6. The model is evaluated based on how well it addresses the defined problem and how well if fits within the design constraints.

7. Branches of engineering include civil, mechanical, electrical, and

© Houghton Mifflin Harcourt Publishing Company

chemical engineering.

8. The engineering design process is used to solve a human problem. Constraints are applied to the design to limit the number of possible solutions.

9. An engineering problem will be easier to solve if the problem is well defined and the constraints are delimited well.

10. The end result of the engineering design process is the development of a new machine, structure, process, or system.

11. Being an iterative process means that the engineering design process is a cycle that is repeated until a satisfactory solution is developed.

12. If no solution is found that adequately solves a problem and meets all design constraints, then engineers could either identify the problem in different terms or change or relax some of the constraints.

13. B

How Are Engineering Design Solutions Evaluated? ETS1.C

1. prototype
2. engineering design process
3. constraints
4. pulleys, levers
5. identifying, researching
6. iterative
7. problems
8. Engineers find the optimal solution by repeating the design, test, and evaluate steps. Each time, the design better solves the problem and meets more of the constraints. Eventually, the engineers find what they deem to be the optimal solution.
9. Promising solutions that are developed into model or prototypes are tested and evaluated against the problem statement and design constraints. Changes are made and the model is redesigned, rebuilt, retested, and reevaluated. This process continues until an optimal

solution is found.

10. Pulleys and levers are examples of engineering solutions that humans have been using for thousands of years.

11. Testing and evaluating a design must be an orderly process because identifying the optimal solution will require organized data and a systematic evaluation of advantages and disadvantages of each solution.

12. Possible answer: If engineers found two designs that equally solved the problem and met all current constraints, they may analyze the problem to determine if any other constraints exist that could be used to decide between the two designs.

13. C

© Houghton Mifflin Harcourt Publishing Company